W9-CER-056

DATE DUE

Child

Welfare

OPPOSING VIEWPOINTS®

OTHER BOOKS OF RELATED INTEREST

OPPOSING VIEWPOINTS SERIES

Abortion
Adoption
American Values
America's Children
Child Abuse
Education in America
The Family
Gangs
Interracial America
Juvenile Crime
Poverty
Sports in America
Suicide
Teenage Pregnancy
Teenage Sexuality
Welfare
Work
Working Women

CURRENT CONTROVERSIES SERIES

The Abortion Controversy
Family Violence
Gay Rights
Hunger
Marriage and Divorce
Smoking
Teen Addiction
Youth Violence

AT ISSUE SERIES

Child Sexual Abuse
Single-Parent Families
Smoking
Welfare Reform

Child

OPPOSING VIEWPOINTS®

Welfare

David L. Bender, *Publisher*

Bruno Leone, *Executive Editor*

Brenda Stalcup, *Managing Editor*

Scott Barbour, *Senior Editor*

Carol Wekesser, *Book Editor*

OPPOSING
VIEWPOINTS®
SERIES

Greenhaven Press, Inc., San Diego, California

Cover photo: Craig MacLain

Library of Congress Cataloging-in-Publication Data

Child welfare : opposing viewpoints / Carol Wekesser, book editor.
      p.   cm. — (Opposing viewpoints series)
      Includes bibliographical references and index.
      ISBN 1-56510-679-2 (lib. : alk. paper). — ISBN 1-56510-678-4
(pbk. : alk. paper)
      1. Child welfare—United States. 2. Children—United States—So-
cial condition. I. Wekesser, Carol, 1963– . II. Series: Opposing viewpoints series (Unnumbered)
HV741.C5354 1998
362.7'0973—dc21   97-27518
                                                                          CIP

Greenhaven Press, Inc., P.O. Box 289009
San Diego, CA 92198-9009

"CONGRESS SHALL MAKE NO LAW. . . ABRIDGING THE FREEDOM OF SPEECH, OR OF THE PRESS."

First Amendment to the U.S. Constitution

The basic foundation of our democracy is the First Amendment guarantee of freedom of expression. The Opposing Viewpoints Series is dedicated to the concept of this basic freedom and the idea that it is more important to practice it than to enshrine it.

CONTENTS

WHY CONSIDER
OPPOSING VIEWPOINTS?

"The only way in which a human being can make some
approach to knowing the whole of a subject is by hearing
what can be said about it by persons of every variety of
opinion and studying all modes in which it can be looked
at by every character of mind. No wise man ever acquired
his wisdom in any mode but this."

John Stuart Mill

In our media-intensive culture it is not difficult to find differing
opinions. Thousands of newspapers and magazines and dozens
of radio and television talk shows resound with differing points
of view. The difficulty lies in deciding which opinion to agree
with and which "experts" seem the most credible. The more in-
undated we become with differing opinions and claims, the
more essential it is to hone critical reading and thinking skills to
evaluate these ideas. Opposing Viewpoints books address this
problem directly by presenting stimulating debates that can be
used to enhance and teach these skills. The varied opinions con-
tained in each book examine many different aspects of a single
issue. While examining these conveniently edited opposing
views, readers can develop critical thinking skills such as the
ability to compare and contrast authors' credibility, facts, argu-
mentation styles, use of persuasive techniques, and other stylis-
tic tools. In short, the Opposing Viewpoints Series is an ideal
way to attain the higher-level thinking and reading skills so essential in a culture of diverse and contradictory opinions.

In addition to providing a tool for critical thinking, Opposing
Viewpoints books challenge readers to question their own
strongly held opinions and assumptions. Most people form their
opinions on the basis of upbringing, peer pressure, and personal, cultural, or professional bias. By reading carefully bal-
anced opposing views, readers must directly confront new ideas
as well as the opinions of those with whom they disagree. This
is not to simplistically argue that everyone who reads opposing
views will—or should—change his or her opinion. Instead, the
series enhances readers' understanding of their own views by
encouraging confrontation with opposing ideas. Careful examination of others' views can lead to the readers' understanding of
the logical inconsistencies in their own opinions, perspective on

why they hold an opinion, and the consideration of the possibility that their opinion requires further evaluation.

EVALUATING OTHER OPINIONS

To ensure that this type of examination occurs, Opposing Viewpoints books present all types of opinions. Prominent spokespeople on different sides of each issue as well as well-known professionals from many disciplines challenge the reader. An additional goal of the series is to provide a forum for other, less known, or even unpopular viewpoints. The opinion of an ordinary person who has had to make the decision to cut off life support from a terminally ill relative, for example, may be just as valuable and provide just as much insight as a medical ethicist's professional opinion. The editors have two additional purposes in including these less known views. One, the editors encourage readers to respect others' opinions—even when not enhanced by professional credibility. It is only by reading or listening to and objectively evaluating others' ideas that one can determine whether they are worthy of consideration. Two, the inclusion of such viewpoints encourages the important critical thinking skill of objectively evaluating an author's credentials and bias. This evaluation will illuminate an author's reasons for taking a particular stance on an issue and will aid in readers' evaluation of the author's ideas.

As series editors of the Opposing Viewpoints Series, it is our hope that these books will give readers a deeper understanding of the issues debated and an appreciation of the complexity of even seemingly simple issues when good and honest people disagree. This awareness is particularly important in a democratic society such as ours in which people enter into public debate to determine the common good. Those with whom one disagrees should not be regarded as enemies but rather as people whose views deserve careful examination and may shed light on one's own.

Thomas Jefferson once said that "difference of opinion leads to inquiry, and inquiry to truth." Jefferson, a broadly educated man, argued that "if a nation expects to be ignorant and free . . . it expects what never was and never will be." As individuals and as a nation, it is imperative that we consider the opinions of others and examine them with skill and discernment. The Opposing Viewpoints Series is intended to help readers achieve this goal.

David L. Bender & Bruno Leone,
Series Editors

INTRODUCTION

"The inattention to children by our society poses a greater threat to our safety, harmony, and productivity than any external threat."

—Marian Wright Edelman

Children of all ages depend on adults to supply their physical and emotional needs. To ensure that children develop into healthy, well-adjusted adults, society must provide them with adequate food, clothing, shelter, and nurturing. Yet despite the obvious importance of caring for the youngest members of society, many children are left hungry, sick, neglected, and poorly educated. One-fourth of America's children live in poverty. Over three million cases of child abuse and neglect are reported each year. And seventeen million children do not receive the child support that is due to them.

Politicians and pundits disagree about how to address the problems experienced by children. These debates often reflect broad political divisions. Liberals generally advocate government programs such as welfare, housing subsidies, and job training to fight childhood poverty. Liberals are also more likely to favor increased government efforts to prevent child abuse. Conservatives, on the other hand, usually oppose government solutions such as welfare in favor of measures that they believe will strengthen families. For example, they support tax breaks for families with children and proposals to give parents more control over the content of public education.

Discussions about policies that affect children are often highly charged and contentious. According to writer Steven V. Roberts, children "have become stuffed animals in the playpen of American politics, a source of competition, not consensus or cooperation. The left wants more government programs and regulation, the right advocates private solutions and responsibility and neither side sees much virtue in the other's arguments."

This divisiveness is evident in the arguments that liberals and conservatives level at one another's proposals. For example, many liberals view conservatives' call to "strengthen the family" as an attack on nontraditional families—such as those with single, gay, or lesbian parents—or as an attempt to impose conservative or Christian "family values" on society at large. In addition, many liberals believe that conservatives promote "individual responsibility" in order to justify cutting public assistance to poor people. Indeed, a great deal of criticism is directed at conservatives' proposals to reduce or eliminate social programs designed to support poor families with children. In opposing such a plan put forward by conservative social scientist and author Charles Murray, congresswoman and former welfare recipient Lynn Woolsey writes:

> Proposals like that of the social scientist Charles Murray—which would abolish everything from food stamps to subsidized housing—would starve families only to feed alarmist myths about welfare. . . . The denial of essential services would rip the safety net from under families in temporary need and burn the ladder to self-sufficiency for those trapped in long-term poverty.

On the other hand, conservatives are quick to point out flaws in the solutions proposed by liberals. These critics argue that decades of spending government money on programs to fight childhood poverty have not lessened the problem—and may even have exacerbated it. According to Cato Institute scholar Michael Tanner, "There is evidence that welfare itself may prevent people from moving out of poverty. . . . Only 18.3 percent of poor people receiving welfare benefits in 1987 moved out of poverty, while 45 percent of poor people who never received welfare escaped poverty." In light of such statistics, Tanner and other conservatives maintain that rather than helping families become self-sufficient, welfare has made them dependent on the government, thus contributing to the ongoing impoverishment experienced by large numbers of children.

Clearly, children do not benefit when the issues that affect them are reduced to the blaming and partisanship that is often typical of American politics. Moreover, there are positive aspects to both the liberal and conservative agendas and ways in which the two sides can work together to improve the welfare of children. For example, in 1996 both sides worked for welfare reform. While the resulting legislation was controversial, it was a bipartisan effort that many hope will help parents on welfare gradually become independent and able to care for their children on their own.

Various liberal and conservative views regarding children and the problems that confront them are presented in Child Welfare: Opposing Viewpoints, which includes the following chapters: What Are the Causes of the Problems Children Face? What Government Policies Would Improve the Welfare of Children? How Can

Needy Children Best Be Helped? What Can Society Do to Improve the Welfare of Children? Obviously, there is no one solution to the myriad problems that affect America's children. As Marian Wright Edelman, president of the Children's Defense Fund, says, "Jobs, decent education, rebuilding communities, decent role models," and other efforts by both individuals and government will likely be necessary to ensure the future health and happiness of the nation's youngest citizens.

CHAPTER 1

WHAT ARE THE CAUSES OF THE PROBLEMS CHILDREN FACE?

CHAPTER PREFACE

The lives of many of America's children seem bleak when one considers the statistics: One-fourth of American children age six and under live in poverty, almost 30 percent of young children have unmarried parents, the United States ranks thirty-first in its ability to prevent low-birthweight babies and sixteenth in its ability to immunize toddlers for polio, and the rate of homicide among children quadrupled between 1960 and 1991.

It would be overly simplistic to argue that all of these problems—poverty, family instability, poor health care, and crime—have one single cause. The problems that confront children are multifaceted and complex. But identifying a few of the possible reasons for the crises children face may help Americans develop solutions to improve their lives.

For example, many experts focus on the growing rate of out-of-wedlock births as a cause of problems for children. In three decades, the rate of illegitimate births has risen from 5.3 percent to 28 percent. Conservatives such as Charles Murray and William Bennett contend that this rise in illegitimacy has resulted in increasing poverty and other problems for large numbers of children—particularly in the inner cities. According to Murray, "Today's children are too often going malnourished, malnurtured, neglected, and unsocialized . . . because the mother is incompetent and the father is missing altogether."

In contrast, other experts argue that children born to unmarried parents are not necessarily worse off than those born to married parents and that such children should not be maligned with the label "illegitimate." Some maintain that conservatives who target illegitimacy as the source of society's ills are in effect undermining women's right to form nontraditional family arrangements. For instance, author and professor Mimi Abramovitz writes that those who blame out-of-wedlock births for the problems children encounter are simply attacking "the rights of all women . . . to survive outside of the rigid family forms endorsed by the religious right."

Illegitimacy is just one of the many issues experts point to in their efforts to identify the causes of the problems children experience. The following chapter presents debates concerning how illegitimacy, divorce, and unpaid child support affect children.

| "Too many children . . . are being
born to single mothers and absent
fathers."

ILLEGITIMACY IS THE CAUSE OF
PROBLEMS FOR CHILDREN

Charles Murray

Charles Murray is a fellow at the American Enterprise Institute, a
conservative think tank in Washington, D.C. He is the author of
Losing Ground: American Social Policy, 1950–1980 and *In Pursuit: Of Happiness and Good Government*, and he is the coauthor of *The Bell Curve: Intelligence and Class Structure in American Life*. In the following viewpoint, Murray argues that the rise in illegitimate births is the primary cause of childhood poverty and neglect. Reversing this trend of increasing illegitimacy should be the main focus of any social policies aimed at improving the welfare of children, Murray concludes.

As you read, consider the following questions:

1. How does illegitimacy result in the breakdown of families
   and neighborhood institutions, in Murray's opinion?
2. Why is the author not enthusiastic about job training
   programs for people on welfare?
3. According to Murray, how will the debate over the degree to
   which welfare causes illegitimacy be resolved?

From Charles Murray, "Keeping Priorities Straight on Welfare Reform," *Society*, July/
August 1996. Reprinted by permission of Transaction Publishers. Copyright ©1996 by
Transaction Publishers; all rights reserved.

In April 1995 I was asked to testify before the Senate Finance Committee on the welfare reform bill then under discussion. . . . The points I tried to make before the Senate Finance Committee are certainly still pertinent now . . . :

1. *The problem facing America's low-income communities is not that too many women in those communities are on welfare but that too many children in those communities are being born to single mothers and absent fathers.* Reducing illegitimacy is not one of many desirable things to do. It is the prerequisite for rebuilding civic life in low-income black America and for preventing a slide into social chaos in low-income white America.

The debate has kept veering back to an idealized view of "the welfare problem" as one of mothers who are striving hard under difficult circumstances and of children whose primary problem is poverty. Are such women and children an aspect of the problem? Of course. But the dominant reality that should be shaping the welfare debate is that the nation's low-income communities, black and white alike, are increasingly peopled by the grown-up children of unmarried young women and men who were utterly unequipped to be parents. As we have moved into the second, third, and fourth generations of unmarried parenthood, the rest of the networks that once stepped in have also disappeared, for without marriage in one generation, aunts and uncles and grandparents become scarce in the next. As families have broken down, so have the neighborhood institutions for which families are the building blocks.

INCOMPETENT MOTHERS, ABSENT FATHERS

What social workers, pediatricians, and police see today among the children in low-income communities is seldom the age-old ravages of simple poverty. Today's children are too often going malnourished, malnurtured, neglected, and unsocialized not because their parents have no access to material resources but because the mother is incompetent and the father is missing altogether. Whether the mother's incompetence derives from youth, drug addiction, low ability, an unjust social system, or defective character makes little difference to the child. Even that the mother loves the child makes little difference if the love is unaccompanied by the steadfastness, maturity, and understanding of a child's needs that transmute love into nurturing. And finally, the child who grows up without a father in a neighborhood without fathers is at risk in ways that even the most loving and competent mother finds it hard to counter.

2. *The debate about job training and placement for welfare mothers has taken*

on far more importance in the welfare debate than it warrants. The debate about jobs is peripheral because putting welfare mothers to work does nothing to reduce illegitimacy and the problems it causes. Fatherless communities where more of the mothers work are still fatherless communities. The only way that a job program is going to affect illegitimacy is if the work requirement is so harsh and unattractive that it deters pregnancy in the first place. That approach is the antithesis of programs that stress training and help in finding a job. Indeed, the more extensive the job training and placement assistance that is provided to welfare recipients, the more attractive welfare becomes. . . .

ILLEGITIMACY THREATENS WHITES

The overall illegitimacy rate among whites is 22% and growing. . . .

We're all well aware of black illegitimacy, which now stands at 68% and in some cities is over 80%. . . .

Is anyone foolhardy enough to say what happened to blacks cannot happen to whites? White people aren't any more immune to the breakdown in family values and the devastating effects of welfarism than blacks.

Walter E. Williams, *Human Events*, January 21, 1994.

---

3. *Illegitimacy is going to be reduced only by a radical change in the current system, but no one knows quite what that radical change should be.* The states are our only way to find out. Perhaps Governor William Weld is on the right track in Massachusetts. His is not the program I would have designed, but Massachusetts is trying something authentically new, and the only way we will find out whether it works is by waiting to see the results. We already know how wrong the experts can be. Who among the experts predicted that New Jersey's cutoff of $64 of extra support for a second child would have the substantial effects on second births to welfare recipients that Congressional Budget Office Director June O'Neill's work has found? Certainly not I. Certainly not any of the many social scientists who constantly assert that welfare does not encourage births. New Jersey had to go ahead and try before we could know.

Predictably, these findings have already come under attack, underscoring another point: At the end of the day, the debate about the degree to which welfare causes illegitimacy is never going to be resolved by the social scientists. It will only be resolved by states that radically alter the welfare system, including,

I hope, some state somewhere that gets rid of the welfare system altogether. . . .

4. *The choice is not whether to be tough on the parents or compassionate toward their children.* Massive suffering among children is already with us, despite a labyrinth of laws and programs that are supposed to prevent it. You can double welfare, double spending on Head Start, double spending on WIC [Women with Infant Children] and Food Stamps and Medicaid, and that suffering will continue—or increase. If you doubt that, go look up the year when we spent half as much on each of those line items as we do today and compare the plight of children then with the plight of children now. Nor are you engaged in finding some solutions that will cause only good and no harm. Every meaningful reform, including the ones I favor, will cause some children to suffer. So will a continuation of the status quo. This is a necessarily brutal calculation, trying to estimate what strategy will result in the least net suffering. I sympathize with those who find this to be a painful process. No thinking person can find it otherwise. Let me also say frankly that I feel contempt for those who want to pretend that this hard choice is avoidable, who piously urge that we not punish the children for the mistakes of their parents. Millions of children alive today are being punished for the mistakes of their parents, beyond Congress's power to do much about it.

Promoting the nurturing of children and diminishing their suffering must ultimately depend on a wise answer to this question: *How can government policy in a free society make it as likely as possible that children will be born to two mature adults committed to their care?* A debate over welfare legislation that avoids that question, or pretends that it is not central, has failed.

"Conservatives . . . have no right to
punish children for being born into
such a world. But that is just what
their unrelenting and demeaning
attack on 'illegitimacy' intends."

ILLEGITIMACY IS NOT THE CAUSE OF PROBLEMS FOR CHILDREN

Robert Scheer

Many social critics blame poverty and other social ills on the ris-
ing number of out-of-wedlock, or "illegitimate," births. In the
following viewpoint, Robert Scheer decries the use of the word
"illegitimate," calling it a pejorative term that stigmatizes children born out of wedlock. Scheer contends that the increase in
out-of-wedlock childbirth is an unavoidable worldwide phenomenon. Rather than blaming this trend for poverty and other
social problems, he argues, the nation's political leaders should
acknowledge the value of all children—including those born
out of wedlock—and create policies that improve their lives.
Scheer is a contributing editor for the *Los Angeles Times*.

As you read, consider the following questions:
1. What examples does Scheer give of famous people who were
   born out of wedlock?
2. Why is the term "illegitimate" inaccurate, according to
   Scheer?
3. What is the political purpose of stigmatizing out-of-wedlock
   children, in the author's opinion?

From Robert Scheer, "All Children Deserve a Chance," *Los Angeles Times*, September 26,
1995. Reprinted by permission of the author.

For years now I have been paying [California governor] Pete Wilson's salary, and yet this ingrate keeps denigrating me and millions of other taxpayers born out of wedlock as *illegitimate*. This inherently pejorative description is a favorite of conservatives. . . .

Wilson has every right to argue that out-of-wedlock births should be discouraged. Under the best of circumstances, it is harder for a single parent to raise a child, and conditions of poverty can make that task nightmarish. But how does it improve the outlook for such children, their self-esteem, to constantly stigmatize them as *illegitimate* for a decision made by parents before they were born?

Instead, why doesn't Wilson refer to such children as "born out of wedlock," and assure them that they are as legitimate as anyone else in this country, with the same legal rights and entitled to the same opportunities? Why doesn't he remind them that Alexander Hamilton, the principal author of the *Federalist Papers*, which conservatives extol, was born out of wedlock? He can cite a long list of achievers from Desiderius Erasmus to Ella Fitzgerald, Jack Nicholson and Dave Thomas, the founder of Wendy's. Why doesn't he quote the words of Pope John Paul II that "each and every child is a gift from God," a sentiment endorsed by virtually every major religious leader?

COMMON USAGE?

But despite such noble sentiments, the labeling of people as *illegitimate* is acceptable usage even by reporters, columnists and the editors of our leading dictionaries. For example, the Random House unabridged dictionary now blithely offers as the first definition of *illegitimate*: "Born of parents who are not married to each other." That is followed by other definitions "not legitimate, unlawful, illegal," which 20 years ago occupied first place.

When challenged, the editors of dictionaries argue that this is just common usage. But if you look up all the familiar hate words for ethnic and racial groups in the Random House dictionary, you will first be warned that the word in question is "slang; disparaging and offensive." Even WASP, when it refers to a white Anglo Saxon Protestant, carries the same caution. Jesse Jackson was once roundly denounced for referring to Jewish people as "Hymies," but it's somehow acceptable to call him "illegitimate" because his parents weren't married.

The word *illegitimate* is not only "disparaging and offensive" but it is also inaccurate. What law have we broken? True, there was a time in English common law when we were a despised subcategory of the population with severely limited legal rights particularly as to inheritance. But that is no longer the case, even in England. At 31%, their rate of out-of-wedlock births is actually higher than in this country. England finally had the good sense in 1987 to pass the Family Law Reform Act, which formally ended the distinction between *legitimate* and *illegitimate* children.

OUT-OF-WEDLOCK BIRTHS: A WORLDWIDE PHENOMENON

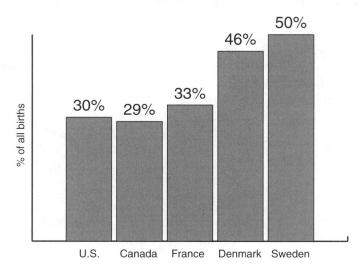

Source: Robert Scheer, *Los Angeles Times*, September 26, 1995.

This is a worldwide phenomenon not tied to the peculiarities of the U.S. welfare system. In the United States, out-of-wedlock births among the poor have leveled off, while the biggest increase of such births has been to women who are professionals and managers. While much has been made of the fact that 30% of births in the United States are out of wedlock, this is not inconsistent with the experience of other Western countries: It is 29% in Canada, 33% in France, 46% in Denmark and 50% in Sweden.

STIGMATIZING CHILDREN

Conservatives can bemoan this changed reality, but they have no right to punish children for being born into such a world. But that is just what their unrelenting and demeaning attack on "illegitimacy" intends. William Bennett, the self-proclaimed keeper of virtue, has said openly that he wants "greater social stigma" to be attached to "illegitimacy." But who is being stigmatized? Not the parents, particularly the fathers, who often disown the children, but rather the children themselves. What is the virtue in slandering them?

The political purpose, not the virtue, is clear. At a time when the welfare system is to be eliminated without any serious thought as to what will replace it, it is politically expedient to dismiss the children supported by that program as expendable. Once labeled as *illegitimate*, they can be dismissed as counterproductive from birth. If we think of them as throwaway children, then undermining their life support system does not suggest a societal loss.

That is an ugly thought, and it is time for the millions of us who surmounted such adversity and now help pay the government's bills to provide witness that this attitude is not only heartless, but also factually wrong.

| "A mountain of psychological research shows that divorce injures . . . children psychologically."

DIVORCE HARMS CHILDREN

Steven Waldman

In the following viewpoint, Steven Waldman maintains that many children are severely harmed when their parents divorce. He contends that divorce negatively affects how children perform in school and how well they will do as adults in the workplace and in relationships. Waldman advocates making divorce more difficult for couples with children to obtain and bringing back the concept that divorce is shameful and undesirable. Waldman is a contributing editor for the *Washington Monthly*, a journal of social and political commentary.

As you read, consider the following questions:

1. What proportion of marriages end in divorce, according to the author?
2. What are the three reasons given by the author for why there is little debate about divorce?
3. Who does Waldman believe should be praised for getting divorced?

From Steven Waldman, "The Case Against Divorce," *Washington Monthly*, January/February 1997. Reprinted with permission from the *Washington Monthly*. Copyright by The Washington Monthly Company, 1611 Connecticut Ave. NW, Washington, DC 20009, (202) 462-0128.

When politicians debate the causes of the family breakup in the inner city, they never mention this statistical couplet: While the rate of out-of-wedlock births nearly doubled in the 1980s, the rate of divorce nearly doubled in the 1970s. I can't prove that the liberalization of divorce laws caused the surge of illegitimacy among the poor, but clearly it was the middle class that led the assault on the "sanctity" of marriage.

It's hard to think of a social phenomenon more harmful, and less discussed, than divorce. More than half of marriages end in divorce, and a mountain of psychological research shows that divorce injures women especially financially and children psychologically. Many argue that divorce cannot be as bad for kids as living in a home with parents who hate each other, but Bill Galston of the Progressive Policy Institute recently summarized the social science literature on this question: "Divorce itself [as opposed to the bad relationship] has an independent negative effect on the well-being of minor children . . . in areas such as the following: school performance, high school completion, college attendance and graduation, labor-force attachment and stable work patterns, crime, depression, psychological illness, suicide, out-of-wedlock birth, and the propensity of children of divorce to become divorced in turn." We think of welfare kids as uniquely estranged from their fathers, but 40 percent of children of divorce have not seen their dad in the past year.

TOO CLOSE FOR COMFORT

Yet politicians hardly ever talk about divorce. Why? In part it's because they understand the subject too well. Politicians ranging from Ronald Reagan to Ted Kennedy—as well as journalists like Peter Jennings and Sam Donaldson—have been through it themselves. Those of us who haven't know someone who has. We understand the tragic circumstances that can lead to the breakup of a marriage. In other words, we are far less likely to be judgmental about divorce than about, say, teenage pregnancy, a subject that, for most of us, is entirely abstract.

Another reason there is so little debate is that the rise of divorce was, in part, a response to a very real problem. Before the 1960s, women had trouble escaping from constraining or abusive marriages. Countless millions were subjected to lives of misery because they couldn't or wouldn't get out of horrible marriages. No one wants to go back to the old days, and criticism of divorce should not be viewed as a fundamental attack on feminism or women's rights. But feminists need to concede that the current situation is unacceptable, too.

26

Finally, this problem is ignored because the solutions aren't obvious. Galston proposes that we should beef up child-support enforcement to at least reduce the financial disruption. Some evidence suggests that fathers forced into making financial contributions tend to demand more of a relationship with their children. Galston also argues that divorce laws should err on the side of keeping minor children in their pre-divorce residences and communities.

The "Rall" cartoon by Ted Rall is reprinted by permission of Chronicle Features, San Francisco.

The key is to draw a much clearer distinction between divorces that involve kids and those that don't. In fact, divorce among childless adults should be even easier, to reduce the odds of a baby being born into a disintegrating family. But divorce among couples with children should be harder. Too often, parents fail to look beyond their selfish needs; they should have to prove that separation is good not only for the adults but for the kids. Perhaps waiting periods or counseling requirements would mitigate the damage to children.

BRINGING BACK THE STIGMA

Most importantly, society has to offer clearer messages about what is shameful and what isn't. Casual divorce should be disparaged as much as casual sex. Pundits who reminisce about restoring the stigma to out-of-wedlock births might remember that divorce used to be considered dishonorable too. (In a

Newsweek piece on this subject, Bill Turque recalls the 1952 *Look* magazine article about Adlai Stevenson: "Can a Divorced Man be Elected President?") If Bill Clinton screwing around on his wife was a legitimate character issue, then so too was Reagan's divorce from Jane Wyman after they'd had children.

At the same time, we should heap praise on couples that split up without having kids; by going through a small ordeal now, they've prevented a much greater future tragedy. Conversely, some parents who stay together for the kids' sake should be considered heroes. The message should be everywhere—on TV shows, in the psychologist's office, and at the holiday dinner table—that while it often takes "strength" to leave a bad marriage, it takes courage and maturity to put the happiness of your children before your own.

To be sure, there are some times when divorce really is best for the kids. And it's very hard for any individual, let alone a lawmaker, to make sweeping conclusions about someone else's marriage. But at least a public debate about divorce might guilt trip some parents into putting the needs of their kids first.

"Several studies . . . have shown that parental conflict—more than family structure—is to blame for the emotional and psychological problems of children of divorce."

DIVORCE NEED NOT HARM CHILDREN

Randall Edwards

Many psychologists and social scientists have reported that children whose parents divorce are more likely than others to experience emotional and psychological problems such as depression, poor school performance, and delinquency. In the following viewpoint, Randall Edwards contends that these problems result not from the breakups themselves but from the parental conflicts that precede and follow divorce. He insists that the harms of divorce can be avoided if divorcing parents cooperate to minimize conflict and ensure that their children maintain strong relationships with both parents. Edwards is a freelance writer and reporter.

As you read, consider the following questions:

1. In the study by Constance R. Ahrons, as cited by Edwards, what proportion of families established cooperative postdivorce relationships?
2. According to Jack Arbuthnot, quoted by the author, what is the "main predictor of a child's ability to survive a divorce"?
3. What conclusion does Constance R. Ahrons draw from divorce trends since the Industrial Revolution, as cited by Edwards?

Adapted from Randall Edwards, "Healthy Divorces Can Lead to Well-Adjusted Children," *APA Monitor*, February 1995. Copyright ©1995 by the American Psychological Association. Adapted with permission.

Contentious divorces are out; mediation is in. Custody "battles" are considered bad form; civilized couples sign "shared-parenting" agreements. Anger, hurt and bitterness are still common themes in most crumbling marriages, but divorced and divorcing parents finally may be learning what psychologists have been saying for years: Fighting over children is a sure way to psychologically damage them.

Several studies assessing the long-term impact of divorce on families have shown that parental conflict—more than family structure—is to blame for the emotional and psychological problems of children of divorce. In many cases, adjustment problems were reported in children long before the parents divorced.

AMICABLE DIVORCE

Psychologist Constance R. Ahrons, PhD, believes parents can divorce without scarring their children if they avoid loyalty conflicts. A "civil, well-functioning, two-parent family" is a realistic goal, she writes in her 1994 book, *The Good Divorce*. Ahrons is a professor of sociology at the University of Southern California.

In fact, amicable divorces are more common than people realize, Ahrons said. In a five-year study of 98 divorced families, Ahrons discovered that about half the families overcame the adversarial legal process of divorce to fashion postdivorce families that ranged from civil to very friendly.

The families in her study were predominantly white and middle-class from Dane County, Wisconsin, selected from divorce court records, not clinical caseloads. The study began in 1989 and involved face-to-face interviews with both partners one year after the divorce.

She found that fathers who remained emotionally involved with their children have more cooperative relationships with ex-wives and are more likely to be current on child-support obligations. The ultimate measure of a good divorce, she said, is how the children are doing—"whether they can have a good relationship with both parents . . . as free from conflict as possible."

AVOIDING THE PITFALLS

Ahrons believes that amicable divorces are possible, if couples:

• *Change the way they think about divorce.* People should stop assuming divorce is bad and destroys children, and begin thinking in terms of a "binuclear family."

• *Stay in charge.* Couples shouldn't let lawyers and judges make the decisions, or escalate conflicts.

• *Slow down the process.* Therapists can help the spouse who wants to end the relationship recognize that the spouse being left needs time to assimilate the changes in his or her life.

• *Recognize children's basic rights to interact with both parents,* except in cases of abuse or neglect.

• *Give themselves a chance to grieve.* Much of the anger characteristic in divorce is expressed to ward off hurt and feelings of loss, by both sides. Ahrons supports divorce rituals, such as the returning of wedding rings, or simply a conference with close friends and family to discuss the end of the marriage. "It is very, very rare that there is a marriage that is all bad. It's full of ambiguities, and those will remain unless we go through some sort of grieving together."

A Child's Survival

The main predictor of a child's ability to survive a divorce is the amount of conflict involved, said Jack Arbuthnot, PhD.

"Not just the conflict during the divorce, but the amount of conflict leading up to it, and continuing afterward," said Arbuthnot, a professor of psychology at Ohio University and co-director of the Center for Divorce Education. The center is an independent research and training organization that provides educational materials and programs for children and parents of divorce.

A Harmonious Environment Is Best

Although people often have been brought up to believe that parents should stay together for the sake of the children, research does not support this belief. It is not in the children's best interests for unhappily married couples to stay together when this exposes their children to chronic marital conflict. Researchers have shown that children adjust better in split homes that function well than in conflict-ridden marriages. More specifically, a harmonious intact family is best for children, but a harmonious divorced environment is better than a disharmonious intact family.

Edward Teyber, *Helping Children Cope with Divorce*, 1992.

Its video program "Children in the Middle" is used in mandatory parent-education classes in 300 domestic relations courts across the country. The program, which attempts to persuade parents to adopt cooperative parenting strategies after divorce, has been successful, Arbuthnot said, although judicial acceptance has been slow.

Courts that have used the program have noticed a dramatic

decrease in postdivorce litigation if parents take the class within 30 days of filing for divorce. If they don't participate in such an intervention, "the whole purpose of going to court [becomes] trash[ing] the other parent," Arbuthnot said. "Parents involved in litigation become increasingly more angry and more polarized."

Arbuthnot said courts should encourage shared parenting plans that distribute the burdens and joys of parenting evenly, even if there is not an exact 50 percent division of time. And parents who do not agree with shared parenting should not be allowed to obstruct such a policy.

It is almost always better for the child to have an active relationship with both parents, he said, "and the kids need to know they can feel comfortable going to visit the other parent."

DIVORCE TRENDS

Arbuthnot and Ahrons have their own irreconcilable differences. Arbuthnot believes even the best-managed divorces create children with problems and, later, adults who have a hard time staying married themselves.

"People get divorced too easily," he said. "There are no societal or family expectations that you tough it out and make it work. I very, very seriously doubt there is such a thing as a good divorce. It's making the best of a bad situation, but that's not a very catchy book title."

Ahrons, on the other hand, argues that divorce trends have been consistent since the Industrial Revolution, and it is time to stop offering societal resistance to divorce. "Divorce is an institution just as marriage is," she said. "There is no indication that it is going to shift. And we're only making it harder on people when we don't accept it."

"Every day in the United States, more than 17 million children struggle to live without the child support they are due."

Unpaid Child Support Harms Children

Richard "Casey" Hoffman

Richard "Casey" Hoffman was the director of the Texas child support program from 1986 to 1991. He is currently the president of Child Support Enforcement, an Austin, Texas, company that collects child support for clients. In the following two-part viewpoint, Hoffman argues that the failure of noncustodial parents—especially fathers—to pay court-ordered child support for their children contributes to the poverty experienced by millions of American children. In Part I, he contends that men must put pressure on one another to accept responsibility for the financial support of their children. In Part II, he calls for increased enforcement of federal child-support laws. These efforts are needed, Hoffman maintains, in order to improve the welfare of the nation's children.

As you read, consider the following questions:

1. What percentage of mothers who are eligible for child support receive payments, according to Hoffman?
2. Why must society rely on men's voluntary compliance with child support laws, in the author's opinion?
3. According to Hoffman, what was the Child Support Recovery Act designed to accomplish?

Part I: From Casey Hoffman, "Social Pressure Can Boost Child Support," *Dallas Morning News*, May 31, 1996. Reprinted by permission of the author. Part II: Richard "Casey" Hoffman, "Not Enough Teeth in Deadbeat Law," *Chicago Sun-Times*, April 27, 1996. Reprinted by permission of the author.

I

On Saturday [June 1, 1996], thousands of people will gather at the Lincoln Memorial in Washington to put pressure on government, business, and cultural leaders to make children and family issues a national priority.

But will the men of America be at the "Stand for Children," an event being sponsored by more than 1,500 organizations?

Will they seek the camaraderie that was displayed at 1995's Million Man March?

Will they finally make a commitment—publicly and personally—to support their children?

Every day in the United States, more than 17 million children struggle to live without the child support they are due. That adds up to an astounding $34 billion in uncollected support.

Given the wealth that Americans enjoy, how can it be that more than one in five children lives in poverty? One solution is to get tough with parents who don't support their children.

Only 56 percent of the mothers eligible for child support get any help, and only 52 percent of those mothers receive the full amount to which they are entitled.

Since less than 10 percent of the nonpaying parents are women, common sense dictates that the solution to this problem lies in focusing on the men who don't pay.

A Few Ugly Truths

There is no need to turn this national scandal into a sexist fight, but there are a few ugly truths that need to be told.

Men have to stop excusing their lack of responsibility with sayings like, "It is way too much of my income," or "My ex-wife can't manage money," or "She won't use it for the kids."

The time has come for those men to start talking straight and taking action.

Only when men hold one another accountable for their childrens' financial needs will the conspiracy of silence—the wink and the nod—come to an end.

Over the years, men have dominated the institutions that could solve the child support problem. All men—especially legislators, judges, prosecutors, probation officers, child support investigators, and employers—must demand that men provide for the financial support of their children.

The statistics clearly demonstrate that we can't depend on just tough law enforcement. The government-funded child support programs never have collected from more than one in five parents.

Faced with those numbers, it is time to let go of the notion that we will win this war by relying strictly on jail. Instead, we need to focus on voluntary compliance and to take advantage of man's desire not to be despised by his fellow men.

THE IMPORTANCE OF ESTABLISHING PATERNITY

Among the poorest children are the ones born to single mothers. . . . Unmarried mothers have lower child support award rates, less child support paid, and lower likelihood of health insurance in support awards. A major reason for the lack of regular child support is that legal fatherhood has not been established for nonmarital children. And unless paternity is legally established, fathers have no legal responsibility to support them.

Ann Slayton, *Children Today*, vol. 22, no. 1, 1993.

The men dodging their child support obligations should be "called out" by other men as greedy, insensitive, uncaring parents. That will stop the bragging about beating the system.

Only men making demands of other men will raise the expectations we have for the next generation of men—a significant number of whom will end up as single parents.

Men must take a stand for all of the children in this country. They must Stand For Children on Saturday—and every day.

II

Nine out of ten children on welfare are owed child support.

As taxpayers, Americans should be especially alarmed because 40 percent of these children are the responsibility of parents who can support them. Child poverty could be drastically reduced if all child support obligations were met by those who can afford to pay.

The notorious Jerry Nichols—who failed to pay his children $500,000 in support—is undoubtedly one of the most outrageous examples of child support evasion. Unfortunately, the federal government's enforcement of the Nichols case—under the federal Child Support Recovery Act—is a rarity, and comes after a long history of deliberate stonewalling by the U.S. Justice Department.

A MISERABLE FAILURE

It has been more than four years since passage of the CSRA, which makes it a federal crime to willfully fail to pay past-due support for more than one year for a child who lives in another state. Once considered a major victory for child support enforcement, the law has failed miserably to live up to its expectations.

The CSRA's failure is largely due to the Justice Department's lack of commitment to the resources to enforce the statute. Since the act's passage in 1992, fewer than 100 cases have been filed.

Every day in the United States more than 17 million children struggle to live without the child support they are due. This adds up to an astounding $34 billion in uncollected support—with one third of these cases being interstate cases.

The CSRA was meant to alleviate these problems by punishing fleeing non-custodial parents who owe more than $5,000 in past child support or who have not paid for more than one year. Non-paying parents face six months' imprisonment and/or a fine.

The act was never intended to cause the U.S. attorney general's office to prosecute all interstate cases. It was designed to encourage U.S. attorneys to pursue a significant number of high-profile cases to send a strong message to all interstate case violators: "If you refuse to pay your child support, you commit a federal crime. You can be found, fined and jailed."

In 1994, Sen. Richard Shelby (D-Ala.), co-author of the CSRA, blasted the federal government's neglect of the act. At that time, only five interstate cases had been filed by U.S. attorneys.

Shelby indignantly chided, "We could significantly reduce child poverty in this country if back child support was paid to the children to whom it is due."

The Senate unanimously passed Shelby's amendment instructing U.S. Attorney General Janet Reno to immediately step up the enforcement of CSRA cases. Only after this "unified, bipartisan wake-up call" did the Justice Department begin to take steps.

Years later, the bill still sits on the books virtually unused. It is not hard to discover why.

From the time the law first passed, the attorney general adopted policies that discourage cases from ever reaching the office of the U.S. attorneys. The cases that do reach the U.S. attorneys in each state are placed at the very bottom of the priorities list.

Reno needs to announce how vigorously her department will prosecute CSRA cases, so we can measure how effectively they meet their goals. She should immediately direct all U.S. attorneys to make CSRA cases a priority, and assign the necessary staff to work exclusively on child support cases.

The U.S. Justice Department must stop paying lip service to child support enforcement and do what Congress ordered.

To do less is disingenuous. To do less perpetuates this crime against society. To do less allows this victimization of children to continue.

"The vast majority of noncustodial fathers DO pay child support. Many who don't pay simply don't have the money."

THE PROBLEM OF UNPAID CHILD SUPPORT IS EXAGGERATED

Part I: Jeffery M. Leving, Part II: Kathleen Parker

In the following two-part viewpoint, Jeffery M. Leving and Kathleen Parker argue that the problem of "deadbeat dads"—fathers who do not make court-ordered child support payments—has been overstated by policy makers and the media. Many so-called deadbeat dads are actually concerned fathers who are financially unable to make their child support payments, the authors contend. In addition, they insist, many fathers are discouraged from making payments because their visitation and custody rights are restricted. Rather than cracking down on deadbeat dads, Leving and Parker maintain, society should allow divorced fathers to remain involved in the lives of their children. Leving is a matrimonial lawyer in Chicago and coauthor of the book *Fathers' Rights*. Parker is a columnist for the *Orlando (Fla.) Sentinel*.

As you read, consider the following questions:

1. What does Leving mean by the "hostile cycle of money versus visits" that occurs after divorce?
2. What percentage of fathers with joint custody pay their child support, according to the Census Bureau statistics cited by Leving?
3. What percentage of children live without their biological father, according to Parker?

I

A ndy Duncan, a divorced father of two living in Gardner, Kansas, had fallen on hard times. He had lost his job as a commodities broker and was having trouble keeping up with his child-support payments. One weekend, he arrived at his ex-wife's Nebraska home to pick up his kids for their court-ordered visit and found no one there. His wife later informed him that, since he was behind on his payments, he would not be seeing his kids. As he struggled to meet his obligations, his ex continued to prevent his visits. When Duncan went to court, his wife was fined $200 for interfering with his visits; he was jailed for nonsupport.

Such unequal justice is common. As a matrimonial lawyer, I've been able to see firsthand how willing most people—judges included—are to brand a "deadbeat dad" as one of the lowest forms of life on earth. All 50 states enforce tough acts to garnish his wages and throw him in jail. And, certainly, any man who refuses to help support his children is wrong, and any mother has the right to pursue every legal avenue to collect.

A Hostile Cycle

But is the father a rotten parent? Not always: Some fathers, like Duncan, *can't* pay. And many others are withholding payments because the mothers—frustrated by the same adversarial legal system—withhold or limit visitation.

Once this hostile cycle of money versus visits starts, the children are the losers every single time: They lose by missing out on a full relationship with their father and by being manipulated by their mother—and they lose financially because the more estranged the father feels, the less likely he is to keep up payments.

In a divorce, the answers are seldom easy, but they are clear. To preserve the family—divorced or not—courts must protect the father-child relationship. Kids need so much more from a dad than his money; courts can only hurt families by sending the message that to be a good father, all he need do is pay up on time.

So how *do* we get dads to pay? Vilifying the so-called deadbeats isn't the answer, even though legislators seem to have decided that punitive action is the best way to go. But those well-publicized crackdowns yield poor results: From 1995 to 1997, Florida arrested more than 5,000 offenders in its Operation Non-Support. So far it has raised only $576 per arrest.

Besides, while threatening a man with jail time will demoralize him, it will only serve to further distance him from his children, both physically and emotionally, and it certainly doesn't improve the odds of his paying.

The Answer: Joint Custody

So what will bring him closer to the children, make him more involved in their lives, and therefore more likely to hold up his end financially? Joint custody, whenever a judge thinks it possible. In these arrangements, both parents have a say in decisions that affect their child's welfare. A 1995 Census Bureau study found that an astounding 85 percent of noncustodial fathers with joint custody paid all or part of child support due, compared with 79 percent of fathers who had only visitation privileges and 56 percent of fathers who had neither visitation nor joint custody. The implication is obvious: Fathers who are active participants in their children's lives are far more likely to be financially responsible too.

The courts should be deeply concerned about gender bias and its damaging effects on children. Our society's foundation, and the emotional health of our children, depend on it.

II

"You can't open a newspaper these days without reading about America's couple du jour: Deadbeat Dad and Welfare Mom. They're the bane of moral America, metaphor for our nation's declining families, political scapegoats for everything from the national deficit to teen violence.

The solution to our problems is crystal clear, to hear our leaders talk. Track down the deadbeats, make them pay up, and some 800,000 welfare moms and children magically will be freed from the shackles of poverty and dependency. President Bill Clinton has promised as much along with his vow to track down fathers who've fallen behind in their child-support payments. Meanwhile, state attorney generals around the country are posting "wanted" fliers of deadbeat dads on courthouse walls and on the Internet, as well as garnishing wages, throwing fathers in jail and, in some cases, revoking drivers' licenses.

Who are these dastardly deadbeats anyway? They're probably lolling around some Caribbean beach as we speak, sipping frozen daiquiris from pineapple shells while bikini-clad native girls massage their feet. Such is the stereotypical image that comes to mind as we ponder the irascible deadbeat dad—a man who has abandoned his family to pursue broader interests.

We need only recall Jeffrey Nichols—the $300,000-a-year precious metals expert who didn't support his kids—to feel smugly self-righteous in our pursuit of these scoundrels. The problem is, most deadbeats aren't like Nichols. Most are more like William Koontz, a Clarence, MO factory worker who earns $15,000 a year and owes $96,000 in back child support. Koontz's wages now are being garnished to the tune of $140 per week to reimburse the state of Florida for money it paid Koontz's ex-wife to support their two children. His new family, meanwhile, is on food stamps.

UNFAIR LYNCHINGS

Those weary of government handouts are pleased to applaud government action that exacts greater responsibility from parents. Yet, there's the nagging sense that not all financially strapped dads are malicious or neglectful, and that these symbolic public lynchings in some cases may be unfair.

Gerald Rowles, head of DADI (Dads Against the Divorce Industry), analyzed Iowa's recently unveiled deadbeat dad poster comprised of men who habitually had disregarded court orders. Nine of the 11 are twentysomething, blue-collar construction or low-income workers earning annual salaries of about $16,000.

A MISTAKEN NOTION

In 1992 the Institute for Research on Poverty at the University of Wisconsin found that 52 percent of obligors who are delinquent in their child support payments earn less than $6155 per year. That's not enough to support one person. And in a report by the General Accounting Office, 66 percent of mothers who do not receive support report that the fathers cannot afford to pay the support ordered. (The report also found that up to 14 percent of child-support obligors are deceased.)

Other government reports show that when there are court orders for support, 76 percent of fathers pay. According to Justice Department statistics, there are about 950,000 men in state and federal prisons. A survey of these inmates found that 76 percent of federal prisoners and 64 percent of state prisoners have one or more children. And there are thousands of men in mental institutions, drug rehab centers and homeless shelters. When you consider the number of unemployed, disabled or ill, the portrait of the deadbeat dad as callous falls apart.

Stuart Miller and Armin Brott, *Playboy*, February 1996.

"My suspicion," says Rowles, "is that most of these guys don't even know that a court-order has been issued." Meanwhile, all have been found guilty in the public eye if not by a court with no consideration of possible extenuating circumstances.

No one's trying to raise the status of deadbeat dad to martyr, but the current political fervor radiates the indiscriminate heat of a lynch mob. The truth is that the vast majority of non-custodial fathers DO pay child support. Many who don't pay simply don't have the money. The federal government says 66 percent of non-payments are due to "financial inability."

FATHERS ARE DISENFRANCHISED

In other cases, fathers don't pay because they've been alienated from their children, often not by choice. According to the Census Bureau 90 percent of fathers awarded joint custody pay their child support. Of those with visitation rights, 79 percent pay. Of those fathers with no visitation, only 45 percent meet their child-support obligations.

In other words, men who don't get to see their children tend to move on, a fact that may not be morally defensible, but which nonetheless is humanly understandable.

It seems that if we're really interested in protecting children rather than in seeking revenge or increasing political leverage, we might do better to stop slapping fathers' faces on wanted posters and focus on the underlying problem, which seems obvious.

For a variety of reasons, fathers increasingly feel disenfranchised from their children. It is nearly axiomatic that with disenfranchisement comes dereliction of duty. The solution to deadbeat dads isn't criminalizing fathers, but allowing them to be part of their children's lives. Tonight, in a nation where fatherlessness is recognized as one of our most serious social problems, 42 percent of all children will sleep in a house where their biological father does NOT live.

The wonder isn't that we have deadbeat dads, but that we don't have more.

Sure, some of the deadbeats are low-lifes who don't care about their kids. In every town and country, a certain percentage of men and women are irredeemable scumbags. But it's surely unfair and unproductive to label every father who falls behind in his child support payments a "deadbeat dad." It's also not a very nice message to send to his children, who, you can be certain, already have suffered enough.

PERIODICAL BIBLIOGRAPHY

The following articles have been selected to supplement the diverse views presented in this chapter. Addresses are provided for periodicals not indexed in the *Readers' Guide to Periodical Literature*, the *Alternative Press Index*, the *Social Sciences Index*, or the *Index to Legal Periodicals and Books*.

Joseph Adelson	"Splitting Up," *Commentary*, September 1996.
Peter Applebome	"Study Says Society Fails 19 Million Youths," *New York Times*, October 12, 1995.
Keith Bradsher	"Poor Children in U.S. Are Among Worst Off in Study of Eighteen Industrialized Countries," *New York Times*, August 14, 1995.
Susan Chira	"Study Confirms Worst Fears on U.S. Children," *New York Times*, April 12, 1994.
Nancy Dreger	"Divorce and the American Family," *Current Health 2*, November 1996.
Gus Hall	"Capitalism Kills: Profit and Greed Rob Our Children of Their Future," *People's Weekly World*, June 1, 1996. Available from 235 W. 23rd St., New York, NY 10011.
Bill Keller	"As Civil Wars Rage, Children Are Prized for Cannon Fodder," *New York Times*, November 9, 1994.
Michael A. Males	"The Truth About Crime," *Los Angeles Times*, September 15, 1996. Available from Times Mirror Square, Los Angeles, CA 90053.
David Sheff	"If It's Tuesday, It Must Be Dad's House,"*New York Times Magazine*, March 26, 1995.
Lynn Smith	"What's the Matter with Kids Today? Their Parents," *Los Angeles Times*, May 19, 1996.
Margery Stein	"New Creed for Families: I'm Okay, You're Okay," *Insight*, August 8, 1994. Available from 3600 New York Ave. NE, Washington, DC 20002.
John Taylor and Maureen Sherwood	"Divorce Is Good for You/No, It's Not," *Esquire*, May 1997.
Chris Tilly and Randy Albelda	"It's Not Working: Why Many Single Mothers Can't Work Their Way out of Poverty," *Dollars and Sense*, November/December 1994.
James L. Wilks	"Fathers Have Rights, Too," *Essence*, June 1995.

WHAT GOVERNMENT POLICIES WOULD IMPROVE THE WELFARE OF CHILDREN?

CHAPTER PREFACE

During the Great Depression, President Franklin Delano Roosevelt established numerous government programs designed to improve the economy, create jobs for unemployed workers, and provide aid to impoverished citizens. Many of these programs stayed in effect for decades. For example, Aid to Families with Dependent Children (AFDC), created by Roosevelt in 1935 as part of the social security system, lasted until 1996, when it was eliminated as part of a sweeping welfare reform bill signed by President Bill Clinton.

The 1996 welfare reform legislation shifted the responsibility for welfare programs from the federal to the state governments. The states receive block grants from the federal government to use for welfare programs. In exchange, states must, among other things:

- limit welfare benefits to five years for most families
- limit benefits to families in which the head of the household remains unemployed after two years
- work to reduce the number of illegitimate births.

Clinton describes the reform as a way "to make welfare what it was meant to be: a second chance, not a way of life." Clinton and others, particularly conservatives, argue that the system initiated by Roosevelt had become counterproductive. Rather than providing a means for poor people to become self-sufficient, critics maintain, the welfare system made them dependent on the government for subsistence. Commentators insist that this reliance on government aid has contributed to the impoverished conditions endured by many inner-city children, who are at risk of becoming welfare recipients themselves.

On the other hand, critics contend that under the welfare reform law many children will be deprived of food, clothing, shelter, and health care. The federal Office of Management and Budget estimated in 1996 that one million additional children would be pushed into poverty by the reform. According to social policy professor and author Mimi Abramovitz, welfare reform "harms poor women and their children first and foremost for being poor. . . . The deprivations of poverty, not the receipt of a welfare check, impair children's development on all fronts."

The authors in the following chapter debate the proper role of government in helping poor children and discuss the effects of government programs on children and their parents.

"The 'nanny state' has eroded self-reliance and encouraged dependency."

WELFARE REFORM WILL BENEFIT CHILDREN

William J. Bennett

In August 1996, President Bill Clinton signed a comprehensive welfare reform bill. Among other measures, the legislation eliminated the federal program Aid to Families with Dependent Children (AFDC) and replaced it with grants for the states to devise their own antipoverty programs. In addition, it called for the enforcement of state child-support laws and gave the states the option of denying additional benefits to recipients who have additional children. In the following viewpoint, written prior to the bill's passage, William J. Bennett advocates these reforms as a means of eliminating the "cycle of welfare" that he believes has resulted in numerous problems for children—especially in the inner cities. Bennett is the codirector of Empower America, a public policy research organization in Washington, D.C., and the author of several books, including The Book of Virtues and The Devaluing of America: The Fight for Our Culture and Our Children.

As you read, consider the following questions:

1. What are some of the "real-world" facts Bennett cites to illustrate the condition of American children?
2. What, in the author's opinion, is the greatest long-term threat to the well-being of America's children?
3. How does John J. DiIulio, who is quoted by Bennett, describe the environment in which inner-city children grow up?

A t the dawn of the 20th century there was every reason to believe that ours would be (in the title of a best-selling book at the time) "the century of the child." From the early part of the 1900's through the 1950's, despite ups and downs, despite Depression and war, things got better in almost every area touching the welfare of American children: economic security improved, material earnings increased, medicine progressed, family structure was stable, children occupied a valued place in society, and our civic institutions were strong and resilient. In retrospect, it seems as if the midpoint of the century was a high point for the well-being of children.

By the 1960's, however, America began a steep and uninterrupted slide toward what might be called decivilization. Although every stratum of society has been affected, the worst problems have been concentrated within America's inner cities. No age group has remained untouched, but the most punishing blows have been absorbed by children.

In assessing conditions today, it is important to keep perspective: America is not in danger of becoming a third-world country; the vast majority of children do not live in sewers of disease and depravity; and most are not violent, sexually promiscuous, or drug-takers. At the same time, however, there is no question that the condition of too many of our children is not good. The indicators are well-known: low educational achievement, the decline of the two-parent family, moral confusion, and, for a sizable and increasingly large minority, abuse, neglect, and very bleak prospects for the future.

A "TANGLE OF PATHOLOGIES"

Consider some real-world facts:

• From 1960 to 1991, the rate of homicide deaths among children under the age of 19 more than quadrupled. Among black teenagers, homicide is now by far the leading cause of death.

• Since 1965, the juvenile arrest rate for violent crimes has tripled, and the fastest-growing segment of the criminal population is made up of children.

• Since 1960, the rate at which teenagers take their own lives has more than tripled.

• The rate of births to unmarried teenagers has increased by almost 200 percent in three decades; the number of unmarried teenagers getting pregnant has nearly doubled since the mid-1970's.

• Today, 30 percent of all births and almost 70 percent of all black births are illegitimate. By the year 2000, according to the most reliable projections, 40 percent of all American births and 80 percent of all minority births will be out of wedlock.

• During the last 30 years there has been a tripling of the percentage of children living in single-parent families. According to some projections, only 30 percent of white children and only 6 percent of black children born in 1980 will live with both parents through the age of 18.

A useful historical reference point may be 1965, when Daniel P. Moynihan, then an Assistant Secretary of Labor, wrote *The Negro Family: The Case for National Action*. Then, one-quarter of all black children were born out of wedlock; one-half of all black children lived in broken homes at some time before they reached age 18; and 14 percent of black children were on welfare. Moynihan considered this "tangle of pathologies" to be a social catastrophe, and so it was. Today, however, were we to achieve such figures in even one of our major urban centers, we would consider it a stunning accomplishment.

CHILDREN ARE WORSE OFF

As the figures above demonstrate, these problems are by no means limited to lower-class or minority populations. In addition to everything else, divorce, rampant in all social classes, causes over one million children annually to end up, at least temporarily, in single-parent families. And wherever they live, American children today—especially the teenagers among them—spend relatively minuscule amounts of time with either their fathers or their mothers—or their homework—and vastly greater amounts of time on other things, from crime to television.

A few years ago a special commission of political, medical, educational, and business leaders issued a report on the health of America's teenagers titled *Code Blue*. In the words of this report, "Never before has one generation of American teenagers been less healthy, less cared for, or less prepared for life than their parents were at the same age." According to the sociologist David Popenoe, today's generation of children is the first in our nation's history to be less well-off psychologically and socially than its parents.

Nor is the concern limited to the experts. When asked in a recent Family Research Council poll, "Do you think children are generally better off today or worse off than when you were a child?," 60 percent of all Americans—and 77 percent of all black Americans—said children today are "worse off." They are right.

The greatest long-term threat to the well-being of our children is the enfeebled condition—in some sectors of our society, the near-complete collapse—of our character-forming institutions. In a free society, families, schools, and churches have primary responsibility for shaping the moral sensibilities of the young. The influence of these institutions is determinative; when they no longer provide moral instruction or lose their moral authority, there is very little that other auxiliaries—particularly the federal government—can do.

Among those three institutions, the family is preeminent; it is, as Michael Novak of the American Enterprise Institute once famously said, the original and best department of health, education, and welfare. But the family today is an agency in disrepair. Writes David Popenoe:

> This period [the 1960's through the 1990's] has witnessed an unprecedented decline of the family as a social institution. Families have lost functions, social power, and authority over their members. They have grown smaller in size, less stable, and shorter in life span. . . . Moreover, there has been a weakening of child-centeredness in American society and culture. Familism as a cultural value has diminished.

And so, too, has fatherhood. Each night in America, four out of ten children go to sleep without fathers who live in their homes, and upward of 60 percent will spend some major part of their childhood without fathers.

ENCOURAGING THE YOUNG TO DEFER CHILDBEARING

The well-being of American children requires policy changes that not only will reduce illegitimacy and promote marriage, but also will encourage potential parents to defer childbearing until both the mother and the father have acquired the education, job skills, and personal maturity needed to support a family and nurture their children properly. Above all, it is imperative to eliminate the wide array of programs which subsidize and encourage young, poorly educated girls to have children out of wedlock.

Robert Rector, *Issues '96: The Candidate's Briefing Book*, 1996.

In the past, the typical cause of fatherlessness was divorce; its new face is homes headed by never-married mothers. This is "the most socially consequential family trend of our generation" (in the words of David Blankenhorn of the Institute for American Values), and it has seismic social implications. Moynihan warned in 1965 that a society which allows a large number of young men to grow up without fathers in their lives asks for and almost always gets chaos. We have come to the point in

America where we are asking prisons to do for many young boys what fathers used to do.

There are other signs of decay, particularly of the cultural variety. Television shows make a virtue of promiscuity, adultery, homosexuality, and gratuitous acts of violence. Rap music celebrates the abuse and torture of women. Advertisements are increasingly erotic, even perverse. And many of our most successful and critically-acclaimed movies celebrate brutality, casual cruelty, and twisted sex.

A HARSH MORAL UNIVERSE

None of these trends takes place in a moral or cultural vacuum. During the last 30 years we have witnessed a profound shift in public attitudes. The pollster Daniel Yankelovich finds that we Americans now place less value on what we owe others as a matter of moral obligation; less value on sacrifice as a moral good, on social conformity, respectability, and observing the rules; less value on correctness and restraint in matters of physical pleasure and sexuality—and correlatively greater value on things like self-expression, individualism, self-realization, and personal choice. . . .

It would be supererogatory at this late date to catalogue the role of government in giving form and force to these ideas and beliefs through law and policy. Suffice it to say that from the area of criminal justice, to education, to welfare policy, to the arts, to a whole tangle of sexual and family issues, government has increasingly put itself on the side of the forces of decomposition, not on the side of the forces of restoration. The consequence is that the moral universe we are sending our children into today is more harsh, more vulgar, more coarse, and more violent than the moral universe most of us grew up in—and they are less equipped to deal with it.

We should not flinch from admitting this unsettling truth: we live in a culture which seems dedicated to the corruption of the young, to assuring the loss of their innocence before their time. "It dawned on me recently," the anthropologist David Murray has written, "that we have now become the kind of society that in the 19th century almost every Christian denomination felt compelled to missionize."

THE NANNY STATE

If the problem is one of moral breakdown, it would be fatuous to suggest that it can be fixed by government intervention. There is, after all, one proposition which has been tested repeatedly over the last three decades and just as repeatedly been found wanting—namely, that we can spend our way out of our social problems. Instead of encouraging government, we need to relimit it—not only, or even primarily, for fiscal reasons, but because the "nanny state" has eroded self-reliance and encouraged dependency, crowding out the character-forming institutions and enfeebling us as citizens.

Still, there are a number of actions government *can* take that would amount to constructive and far-reaching, even radical, reforms. A number of these ideas have been on the table for quite some time, but as the results of the November 1994 elections [in which Republicans won majorities in both houses of Congress] suggest, Americans may be more ready for fundamental reform today than at any other point in recent history. So we suddenly find ourselves presented with an extraordinary opportunity.

Before getting down to particulars, I would stipulate two general points that should guide any discussion of public-policy solutions to the problems faced by children in America. One of them I borrow from an old principle of medicine: *primum non nocere*—first, do no harm. In many, many cases, the best thing government can do is (to quote Myron Magnet of the *City Journal*) "to *stop* doing what makes the problem worse."

As for the second point, it was well expressed by Alexander Hamilton, who in *The Federalist No. 17* questioned whether "all those things . . . which are proper to be provided for by local legislation [should] ever be desirable cares of a general jurisdiction." To state this in terms of our present situation, there are many responsibilities which would be better handled by states and localities but which have fallen under the jurisdiction of the federal government; they should be devolved back to the smaller "laboratories of democracy."

WELFARE AND ILLEGITIMACY

Within those constraints, government, at one level or another, does have a role to play in improving conditions for the young. Let us look at . . . the link between welfare and illegitimacy.

Between 1962 and 1992, welfare spending in the United States increased by over 900 percent in 1992 dollars. At the same time, the poverty rate dropped by less than 5 percent— and illegitimacy rates increased over 400 percent. Children are the real victims in this national tragedy. They are being conditioned into the same habits of dependence they are surrounded by, resulting in an almost unbreakable cycle of welfare and "the tangle of pathologies" associated with it.

John J. DiIulio Jr. of Princeton has put this last point well:

> The problem is that inner-city children are trapped in criminogenic homes, schools, and neighborhoods where high numbers of teenagers and adults are no more likely to nurture, teach, and care for children than they are to expose them to neglect, abuse, and violence. . . . Children cannot be socialized by adults who are themselves unsocialized (or worse), families that exist in name only, schools that do not educate, and neighborhoods in which violent and repeat criminals circulate in and out of jail.

Quite a number of serious and thoughtful proposals have been advanced for restructuring the entire system of welfare benefits. . . . I would endorse full-scale and far-reaching plans to send welfare back to the states, which have proved the best settings for innovative reform and experimentation.

As for the problem of illegitimacy in particular, one year after legislation is enacted I would recommend ending direct welfare payments to women who have children out of wedlock; enforcing existing child-support laws; and terminating the increase in benefits for women who have children while participating in welfare programs. The success of such reforms, it seems to me, depends critically on their sweep and magnitude; incremental steps will not do the necessary job of altering fundamental assumptions and expectations. . . .

MORAL AND SPIRITUAL ANSWERS ARE NEEDED

Drawing up laundry lists of public policy may seem a tedious and academic exercise. It is nevertheless an instructive one, if for no other reason than that it glaringly exposes how little has been done, on the most commonsensical level, to address the terrible problems that confront us, and that have accumulated in both number and intensity over the past 30 years. In this sense, thinking concretely about specific, practical reforms offers the hope that, by a concerted national effort, we might yet begin to alleviate some of the worst manifestations of these ills, and even, in time, to reverse course.

And yet, to repeat, even if we were to enact each and every one of the desired reforms in each and every area, we would still be a long way from having healed the broken families of America. Smart, intelligent public policies can and do make a difference. But political solutions are not, ultimately, the answer to problems which are at root moral and spiritual.

"Manners," wrote Edmund Burke two centuries ago,

> are of more importance than laws. Upon them, in a great measure, the laws depend. The law touches us but here and there,

and now and then. Manners are what vex or soothe, corrupt or purify, exalt or debase, barbarize or refine us, by a constant, steady, uniform, insensible operation, like that of the air we breathe in. They give their whole form and color to our lives. According to their quality, they aid morals, they supply them, or they totally destroy them.

Can government supply manners and morals if they are wanting? Of course it cannot. What it can supply, through policy and law, is a vivid sense of what we as a society expect of ourselves, what we hold ourselves responsible for, and what we consider ourselves answerable to. There can be little doubt that in this last period of time the message our laws have been sending our young people and their parents has been the profoundly demoralizing one that we expect little, and hold ourselves answerable for still less.

By changing and improving our laws, we might not thereby bring about, but we would certainly *help* to bring about, a climate that would make it easier rather than harder for all of us to grow more civilized; easier rather than harder for us to keep our commitments to one another; easier rather than harder for us to recapture the idea of personal and civic responsibility. This, in turn, would make it easier rather than harder for us to raise our children in safety to adulthood—something which at the moment we are not doing very well at all.

| "Mothers and children cast off welfare will swell the ranks of the homeless on America's streets."

WELFARE REFORM WILL HARM CHILDREN

Part I: Hugh B. Price, Part II: Thomas J. Osborne

In Part I of the following two-part viewpoint, Hugh B. Price argues that the 1996 welfare reform law will force many women with children off welfare. Due to a dearth of low-skill jobs, he contends, large numbers of these mothers will not find work and will be unable to provide basic necessities for their children. In Part II, Thomas J. Osborne maintains that the welfare reform legislation will push an additional one million children into poverty. He concludes that the United States should institute a more generous welfare system similar to those found in European countries such as France and Italy. Price is the president and CEO of the National Urban League, an organization that combats racial discrimination. Osborne is a history teacher for Rancho Santiago College in Santa Ana, California.

As you read, consider the following questions:

1. What forms of income does Price envision for welfare mothers who are pushed off welfare and cannot find work?
2. According to Price, how should the federal government ensure that there are enough jobs available for former welfare recipients?
3. What did the nonprofit group in Luxembourg conclude regarding poor children in America, as reported by Osborne?

Part I: From Hugh B. Price, "Welfare Reform vs. Welfare Reality," *To Be Equal*, August 2, 1996. Reprinted courtesy of the Urban League, New York, NY Part II: From Thomas J. Osborne, "Civility on Trial: Welfare in the Western World," *Humanist*, January/February 1997. Reprinted by permission of the author.

I

The sweeping legislation overhauling the nation's welfare system that Congress has passed and President Bill Clinton has signed is a calamity. It is a declaration that the federal government has wearied of the war on poverty and decided to wage war against poor mothers and their children instead.

We wholeheartedly endorse the idea that all Americans should earn their keep through gainful employment and entrepreneurship. The core mission of the Urban League movement is helping those we serve become economically self-sufficient.

Superficially, this welfare legislation seems to be consistent with that philosophy. It ends the federal guarantee of public assistance for poor families by imposing a five-year lifetime limit on benefits. This is supposed to push welfare recipients into the labor force by removing the crutch of long-term public assistance.

A SHORTAGE OF JOBS

But the problem is that, while the American economy is a marvel at generating jobs and wealth for the greatest number, it has a rapidly-diminishing number of jobs for those with low skills.

Many inner-city residents simply cannot find work, try as they might, due to the chronic undersupply of low-skill jobs and oversupply of higher-skilled applicants who are willing to compete with low-skill workers for those jobs. Discrimination against black applicants by inner-city and downtown merchants alike is another formidable obstacle to employment.

A study co-authored by Nikolas Theodore of the Chicago Urban League and Virginia Carlson of the University of Wisconsin-Milwaukee found that in Illinois there are four workers in need of entry-level jobs for every job-opening in the state. The problem is worse in the cities: In Chicago, there are six workers for every slot; in East St. Louis, nine.

FAMILY VALUES?

Given that reality, what are welfare mothers who cannot find work supposed to do for family income when the time limits expire? Where will income for rent, heat, clothing, school supplies, and so forth, come from? Do we really want these desperate mothers to turn to hustling, prostitution, drug dealing or panhandling? Are these the family values that Washington has in mind?

Indeed, the Congressional Budget Office in the spring of 1996 warned that many, perhaps even most, welfare recipients who are lopped off the rolls won't be able to find jobs in the private sector. And separate analyses of this legislation by the Urban Institute and the federal Office of Management and Budget indicate that—with one-fifth of America's children already stranded in poverty—it will almost certainly push at least one million more children down to those depths.

Contrary to this bill's assumptions, state governments won't be able to protect these vulnerable citizens because they themselves have significant fiscal problems.

Instead, what is most likely to happen is that mothers and children cast off welfare will swell the ranks of the homeless on America's streets—where their presence will derail the progress many cities have made recently in improving the quality of life of their business districts and neighborhoods.

WELFARE REFORM AND FOSTER CARE

Welfare reform, advocates say, will decimate the already beleaguered foster care system. First, workfare requirements [which require welfare recipients to work] will render foster parents unable to continue taking care of their young charges. Second, as more poor families are kicked off the rolls, they will begin abusing their kids, who in turn will flood a foster care system unprepared for the deluge.

Of all the bad news about welfare reform, the impact on foster care may be the worst news of all.

Adam Fifield and Evan Halper, City Limits, May 1997.

It is imperative that we all speak out, to say that if the federal government really wants to promote self-reliance, instead of washing its hands of the welfare problem, it would, yes, insist that able-bodied welfare recipients work. But it would also fund a public-sector jobs program to re-build the nation's crumbling infrastructure. Such a program would provide work for those where the local unemployment rate is high and there simply aren't enough jobs to go around.

That's what President Clinton originally had in mind when he proposed ending the traditional welfare program. That would be the kind of welfare reform that would truly reflect family values by promoting self-reliance and protecting children.

Unfortunately, the legislation we are now burdened with is just the opposite: It is the action of a Congress and a White House shedding its responsibility to provide for all of the people of the United States, and the nation will soon see its very negative impact.

II

In the Western world, the hot issue of welfare and related social services is being scrutinized by austerity-minded governments. Uncertainty about the security of the working and middle classes abounds. If uncertainty gives way to societal unrest resulting from cutbacks in social spending, we can expect to see an increase in crime, political extremism, and other social pathologies. Depending upon how far the downsizing of Western welfare systems is carried, many on both sides of the Atlantic agree that, on the eve of the twenty-first century, civility itself is on trial.

In order to assess the functioning of welfare systems on the other side of the Atlantic, I spent nearly a month in France and Italy in the summer of 1996 interviewing two dozen government officials, business executives, academicians, journalists, and physicians. When I returned home to California, I compared my findings with recent developments in the welfare controversy in the United States.

THE FRENCH AND ITALIAN WELFARE SYSTEMS

Of the European countries, France has the most complex and certainly one of the most comprehensive social-welfare systems. Nearly 22 percent of the gross national product is spent on welfare—including health, retirement, unemployment, and education—and over half of the GNP is spent on social services overall. France is also burdened with an unemployment level of 12.5 percent (more than double that of the United States) and, like Italy and the United States, it must address the needs of a growing elderly population. The high rate of unemployment is problematic because fewer workers means less government revenue, and in large measure the social-insurance system, especially pensions, is based upon length of employment.

Still, the munificence of France's "womb-to-tomb" social-welfare system is remarkable by any standard. There is comprehensive and largely reimbursable medical and dental coverage. Retired persons receive pension payments of unlimited duration for up to 80 percent of a white-collar worker's final salary and 70 percent for blue-collar workers. The state has mandated an official minimum wage of $1,200 per month, and a minimum of five weeks of paid vacation and two weeks of paid public holidays per year. To help the hard-core unemployed, the government issues *Revenu Minimum d'Insertion* payments ($460 per month for individuals) to poor people over 25 years of age. And, as in many other European countries, there is free education from elementary grades through doctoral and professional programs. Not surprisingly, all of the French people I interviewed gave high marks to their country's welfare system. . . .

The French model of a highly centralized, efficient welfare state contrasts sharply with that of Italy, which is decentralized and loosely organized. Like the French system, however, the Italian system provides national health care, generous unemployment benefits and retirement pensions, and free public education through the university level. Most of Italy's poverty is found in the south, where the unemployment rate is 20 percent and where, according to those I interviewed, welfare fraud is rampant. About 45 percent of the elderly live with and are cared for by their family (the corresponding figure for France is 25 percent). . . .

WELFARE REFORM IN AMERICA

Several days after my return [from Europe], President Bill Clinton signed into law a measure to "end welfare as we know it." This new law abolishes America's 61-year-old commitment to provide cash assistance (through Aid to Families with Dependent Children) to every eligible poor family with children. Through block grants totaling approximately $20 billion annually from the national government, the states will now take over the responsibility for dispensing a reduced amount of federal aid to the needy for up to five years over an individual's lifetime, but no more than two years consecutively. Both food stamps and federal assistance to legal immigrants who have not yet become citizens will be reduced substantially. Washington thereby expects to save $60 billion over six years. A central (and commendable) goal of the "welfare-reform" bill is to move poor people off welfare and into jobs; however, some five million jobs will be necessary to employ all welfare recipients.

Certainly welfare reform was and is needed. If jobs are available, all able-bodied adults of sound mind should work—both for their own good and that of society. But for those unable to earn a living wage or to care for themselves, the new "welfare-reform" law is too draconian, particularly as it relates to children. The Clinton administration estimates that approximately one million more children will slide into poverty with the ending of AFDC, and a year before AFDC was abolished the New York Times published an editorial on the results of a study conducted by a nonprofit group in Luxembourg which stated: "Poor children in America are worse off than poor children in 15 of the 18 Western industrialized countries included in the study."

In early September 1995, liberal Senator Daniel Patrick Moynihan asked his colleagues to picture in their minds what conditions for poor children would be like in ten years if the proposed "welfare-reform" measure passed. He then painted a scenario of people picking up on winter mornings the frozen bodies of youngsters who had fallen asleep on street grates. Shortly afterward, conservative columnist George Will sounded a similar note of disgust in the *Washington Post* regarding the pending bill: "No child is going to be spiritually improved by being collateral damage in a bombardment of severities targeted at adults who may or may not deserve more severe treatment from the welfare system."

A FOREIGN PERSPECTIVE

A foreign perspective on our system is revealing for what it tells us about how our society is perceived by outsiders. Of the 24 people I interviewed in France and Italy, only two thought that the United States had an adequate social-welfare policy. The remaining 22—all of whom said that they liked Americans and admired much about the United States—rated the U.S. social-welfare system as "inadequate" compared to those of Europe. Referring to the United States, Gian Franco Blower, president of Helitalia in Florence, observed: "A rich country socially and culturally cannot afford to not tender to the poor and needy." Barry James, a prominent Paris journalist for the *International Herald Tribune*, told me that, although France would have to reduce social spending, it "would not follow America into abandonment of the poor." Marco Cecchini, a journalist for Italy's largest newspaper, *Corriere della Sera*, who acknowledges the need for cuts in Italy's welfare spending, does not want his country's welfare system "to move in the direction of America's."

Furthermore, nearly all of those I interviewed indicated that they would be afraid to get sick in America because, unless they could afford health insurance, their lives would be at risk. David Elkharrat, a French physician who manages the emergency care facility of a Paris hospital, remarked: "The American system [of health care] is very unfair, and I'm sorry the Clintons did not pass their health-care reform measure. As it stands, if a person in your country is seriously ill, they cannot get health insurance. In France, the more serious your sickness, the more health-insurance coverage you get." Though Europeans may not know that 39 million Americans have no health-care coverage, including 10 million children, they rightly perceive an absence of civility in our health care and other social systems for the disadvantaged.

THE LIMITS OF INDIVIDUALISM

The rolling back of the advances of America's welfare state via the "welfare-reform" measure, says economist Lester C. Thurow of the Massachusetts Institute of Technology, is due largely to our culture of rugged individualism and its attendant emphasis upon near-total personal responsibility for our own fate. Such values and ideas are foreign to many Europeans, who stress the role of economic systems and social injustices in producing poverty.

While in Europe, I got in touch with this country's culture of individualism, risk-taking, and "can-do" attitude by reading excerpts from a biography of Microsoft's cofounder Bill Gates. I found the story of his meteoric rise exhilarating and characteristically American. But at the same time, Gates' type of "turbo-driven capitalism" is leaving millions of our people behind in a dust cloud of poverty. The Twentieth Century Fund recently concluded that one percent of our population owns about 40 percent of the nation's wealth. This disparity might not pose a danger to civil society if we could count on that one percent of "can-do" rugged individualists to provide sufficient jobs, training, and social assistance for all to succeed.

The question I have now is this: can we Americans adapt the European welfare philosophy to our own unique needs in order to share our bounty with those of our fellow citizens who do not have their basic needs met in terms of food, clothing, housing, health care, and education? Just over 60 years ago, an economically depressed America answered with a resounding "Yes!" The result was the establishment of the American welfare state which, with all of its many imperfections, marked the greatest social advancement in our country since the abolition of slavery. For the first time, the federal government committed itself to help those who were least able to help themselves.

As the twenty-first century dawns before us, civility is again being tested throughout the Western world. Demagogues and extremists like those of the 1930s stand ready to exploit impoverished and distressed peoples. Earlier it was Mussolini, Hitler, and Stalin; today their imitators among racist, terrorist, and anti-government groups everywhere feed on the socio-economic discontent of the underclass. The nations of Europe are mindful of this. Not nearly as wealthy as the United States and stretched economically to the limits, they seem determined to keep their welfare and related social programs intact as much as possible. Can America afford to be so uncivil as to ignore their example?

"The Parental Rights and
Responsibilities Act . . . reaffirms
Supreme Court decisions supporting
parents' rights to direct the upbringing
and education of their children."

PARENTAL RIGHTS LAWS WOULD
BENEFIT CHILDREN

Nina Shokraii

In recent years, some state and federal legislators have considered
parental rights legislation as a way of enabling parents to raise
their children free from government interference. These proposed
laws generally state that parents have the right to guide and direct
the education and development of their children. In the following viewpoint, Nina Shokraii supports one such proposal, the
federal Parental Rights and Responsibilities Act (PRRA). Shokraii
contends that the government—particularly the education system—has assumed too large a role in teaching moral values to
the young. She maintains that protecting parents' rights would
help restore parents as the moral educators of their own children.
Shokraii is director of outreach programs for the Institute for Justice in Washington, D.C. Although the PRRA did not pass into law,
some states are considering similar legislation.

As you read, consider the following questions:
1. What specific case does the author cite as an example of
   excessive government interference in the lives of children?
2. How does Shokraii refute the arguments of those who
   oppose parental rights legislation?
3. How do parental rights laws benefit both school districts and
   parents, in the author's opinion?

From Nina Shokraii, "Parents Raise Children, Period," Op-Ed section, *Washington Times*,
April 18, 1996. Reprinted by permission of the *Washington Times*.

John Reinhard is a parent from North Carolina suing his school district for requiring his son, John, to "volunteer" 50 hours of community service prior to graduating from high school. When asked how he could possibly oppose so noble a goal as service to one's community, he replied, "As Ambrose Bierce once noted 'for every problem there is an answer: simple, neat and wrong.' Mandating community service is just such an answer."

Truth is, schools today have become more than the providers of education. Committed to enhancing their students' self-esteem, they have become day care centers, drug-treatment centers and social welfare networks. As Dr. Shirley McCune, a consultant on school restructuring, explained in a 1990 speech, the goal is "to take schools out of the schooling business" and make them "human resource development centers." All Mr. Reinhard wants is for the schools to go back to teaching algebra and reading and to leave the upbringing of his son into a responsible citizen to him and his wife.

NATIONWIDE IMPLICATIONS

Oral arguments for his case were held in Baltimore before the 4th U.S. Circuit Court of Appeals. The suit, *Herndon vs. Chapel Hill-Carrboro City Board of Education*, challenges the district's high school graduation requirement of 50 hours of community service. School districts all across the country are taking up the banner of "mandatory volunteering," so the court ruling could have nationwide implications.

Though he still has an uphill battle ahead, Mr. Reinhard is hopeful that his lawsuit will finally prevail, but what he has gone through thus far is not something many parents will want to endure. In fact, they may not have to if proposed federal legislation called the "Parental Rights and Responsibilities Act," spearheaded in the House by Rep. Steve Largent and in the Senate by Senator Charles Grassley—with the help of the group Of The People—becomes law. . . . When Mr. Reinhard asked the Chapel Hill school board attorney defending against his suit what effect such a law would have on mandatory community service, his response was "the board's case would be gutted if parental rights were fundamental." And cutting back the education establishment's powers over our children's upbringing is exactly what this Congress ought to be focusing on if it is serious about devolving power to families.

Opponents of the Parental Rights Act range from hard-core liberals who believe children are the property of Hillary Clinton's "village," to some advocates of federalism whose goal is merely to shift power back to state and local governments, rather than to individuals. Why, they argue, do we need a federal law empowering parents with the right to raise their children? Both miss the fine balance the Parental Rights and Responsibilities Act strikes: It provides parents with fundamental rights that traditionally and properly are theirs.

PARENTS MUST RETAIN THE AUTHORITY

It is parents—not teachers, child care providers, social workers, or a "village"—that are most likely to give an all-encompassing commitment to the welfare of the child. This is not to denigrate the important work done by teachers, child care providers, and social workers, but simply to acknowledge an important truth: Only parents can reasonably be expected to put the interests of their children above their own. Thus, government must assume that parents, not bureaucrats or politicians, are in the best position to make decisions about their children because only parents can be expected to have this overriding commitment to their children's welfare.

This does not mean that all parents will put their children's interests above their own at all times. Indeed, some parents—especially those who are under the influence of drugs like crack cocaine or alcohol—even abuse their children physically or sexually. In such cases, the state can act to curtail the right of an individual parent or couple to care for a child. But the state can never lawfully curtail the fundamental rights of parents as a class; its duty is to uphold these rights. In all areas of public policy, government should assume that because parents are best able to make decisions about the welfare of their children, they must retain the maximum decision-making authority when it comes to raising those children.

Patrick F. Fagan and Wade F. Horn, *The Heritage Foundation Issue Bulletin*, July 23, 1996.

The Parental Rights and Responsibilities Act does not create, invent or grant any new rights for parents. The act simply reaffirms Supreme Court decisions supporting parents' rights to direct the upbringing and education of their children, while maintaining existing federal and state protections of children from abuse and neglect. This legislation devolves power not just to state and localities, but straight to individuals and parents.

WANTED: A LEVEL PLAYING FIELD

As John Reinhard argues: "Today, parents have no essential rights in the education of their children. Our challenge resembles that of Sisyphus, who forever attempted to roll a boulder uphill only to have the stone roll back down. The non-fundamental rights of parents are our hill and constitute an unlevel playing field in which school boards have the advantage. All we are asking for is to level the playing field." Rather than interfering with local schools by telling them what to teach, the legislation would subject curricula to a necessary standard of scrutiny which has hitherto been lacking. The Parental Rights and Responsibilities Act would turn power away from powerful monied special interests and give it back to the parents.

Under the legislation, parents would not be able to dictate what pupils are taught in the schools nor to interfere with the curriculum choices of public schools. The legislation only protects the right of parents to exempt their children from certain objectionable public school programs, i.e., those that usurp the ability of parents to direct the moral education of their children. Recognizing parental liberty as a fundamental constitutional right serves the school district's interest in promoting educational values while preserving the ability of parents to direct their children's education.

The Parental Rights and Responsibilities Act transfers power from the education bureaucracy and special interests back to parents. In short, it brings parents back into the configuration of the "village." If Republicans are serious about devolution of power, here is one of those rare pieces of legislation on the Hill that does just that.

"These 'parental rights' laws should
be called 'parental rights to abuse'
laws. They give free rein to parents
who shouldn't be parents."

PARENTAL RIGHTS LAWS WOULD
HARM CHILDREN

Bunnie Riedel

Advocates of parental rights legislation believe that such laws
will ensure that parents are free to raise their children as they
wish. In the following viewpoint, Bunnie Riedel refutes this argument. If enacted, she contends, these laws would endanger
children by nullifying thousands of existing laws that enable the
state to protect children from abusive parents. Furthermore,
Riedel insists, parental rights laws would have adverse effects on
public education and other programs that provide essential services for children. Riedel is director of Chapters and Faith
Groups for Americans United for Separation of Church and
State, a Washington, D.C., advocacy group.

As you read, consider the following questions:

1. What does Riedel say is her job as a parent?
2. How would parental rights laws affect education, in the
   author's opinion?
3. To whom does Riedel believe her children "belong"?

From Bunnie Riedel, "A Parent's View of Parental Rights," Christian Social Action, January
1997. Reprinted by permission of Christian Social Action.

When my son was born, I held him in my arms and welcomed him into the world. As I looked into his face bearing that dazed and confused expression so many newborns have, I had an overwhelming sense that this child was mine only "on loan." It was clear to me that he was a separate, distinct, unique individual and that at some point in the future he would make his own way for himself. It was also clear that my job was to give him the best tools I could to prepare him for that time.

Even now, as I raise my children in spurts of teenage frustration and joy, I know that my job is to prepare them to meet the world head-on with as much confidence as possible. It is simply not good enough for them to be molded in an image I might have in my head. They must learn how to think for themselves, make decisions (both good and bad), learn from their mistakes and move into the world as well-rounded human beings with rich experiences to inform their lives. As a parent, it is not easy to let go. However, I know, deep in my heart, that I must let go in stages or my children will never live up to their potential.

It is a constant balancing act between setting up boundaries and limitations that benefit their health and welfare and allowing risks to be taken that will benefit their maturation. It is a frightening thing, and there is not a day that goes by, as they progress toward their lives that are distinct and separate from my own, that I don't say a prayer.

We have great discussions about religion, politics, morality, history and a host of other topics. On more than one occasion, my kids have let it be known that their opinions are very different from my own, and it is fascinating to hear their reasoning. I'm proud that I've taught them how to think through complex problems and come to conclusions, even when those conclusions are not mine. I worry a bit when they sound just like me, because I don't want them just mouthing what they've heard, and I always check to make sure that their opinions are really their own, not just a rehash of mine.

GROWING UP IN AN ABUSIVE HOUSEHOLD

I wasn't raised in such an environment, and it was my upbringing that made me determined that things would be different when I became a parent. I was adopted at the age of two into an extremely abusive household. My adoptive mother raised me in a Pentecostal church, which taught that ideas contrary to what was preached on Sunday morning were products of Satan's influence in the world.

It was not my job to question either the church or my mother.

When I was so foolish as to do so, I was physically beaten. I learned how to keep my thoughts to myself because in my house even thinking was a dangerous thing. That's why I packed a bag and left that house when I was 17, and that's why I've spent a good deal of my life working on issues of conscience.

A Thing Called "Parental Rights"

There is a tremendous amount of talk about a thing called *parental rights*. Parental "rights" legislation is a concoction of the radical Religious Right. The proposals I've seen come across my desk typically say "the state shall not abridge a parent's rights to control or direct the upbringing, education, values and discipline of their children."

These laws sound innocuous enough. No right thinking person would want "Big Brother" poking his nose into every living room in America to interfere with the privacy and sanctity of the family. However, when I dig a little deeper, it becomes clear that the effects of such legislation could be far-reaching in its damage to our society's most vulnerable citizens: children.

Conversations with a wide variety of social service providers suggest that over 2,000 state statutes protecting children would be overturned. If parents are given absolute power to control the upbringing or discipline of their children via statute or state constitutional amendment, the ability of the state to step into abusive situations will be crippled by threat of lawsuit by the parents.

How many times have we read accounts of children forcibly taken from abusive parents and placed into protective custody? Under "parental rights" laws, those abusive parents could suspend the power of the state to intervene on behalf of the abused children. Even as it is now, with the laws that we have, too many children fall through the cracks, and we read about their terrible fates on the front pages of the papers. These "parental rights" laws should be called "parental rights to abuse" laws. They give free rein to parents who shouldn't be parents.

Access to Services Diminished

Even for those children who are not living in physically abusive homes, their access to help and services that they sorely need will be diminished. It is feared that teenagers seeking counseling for birth control or disease prevention will be turned away or forced to obtain parental permission. The effects on these children would be devastating.

I know from talking to my teenagers' friends that so many of them cannot talk to their parents about reproductive health care, and yet, that doesn't stop them from engaging in sexual activity that puts them at risk. The optimum situation is for them to talk to their parents, but if they cannot, then they must be able to seek advice from professionals.

It is now known that the fastest growing population of newly infected HIV patients are teenagers. Are we willing to watch these young people die in their twenties because we were so afraid of lawsuits that we refused them counseling in their teens?

SAFEGUARDS ALREADY EXIST

Parents already have a number of mechanisms they can use in addressing cases where they feel their rights are violated. If they have a complaint with a school, for example, they can take their objections to local newspapers, public officials, school boards, even courts. They can network with other parents. Regardless of the merits of their case, our society offers ample opportunity for the redress of such grievances. Parents and school officials may not always agree with the outcome of such efforts; but imperfect as it may be, our system of local and state education has many built-in safeguards to assure a balance between the "rights" of parents and children, and the interests of educators.

Conrad F. Goeringer, *American Atheist Newsletter,* July 1996.

Closer to home, the parental rights bills would have a devastating effect on education. Since curriculum is considered a "government action," challenges to curriculum would be endless. Imagine the one parent who objects to a social studies curriculum about slavery or maybe a science curriculum involving evolution. Under these laws, any government activity that is found objectionable would have to be suspended while an investigation took place. That means that even if you find the curriculum perfectly suited to your children's needs, your children would be denied that curriculum because an objection had been raised and an investigation was pending. The state would have to prove a compelling reason for continuing the curriculum. Proving compelling interest on the part of the state is very hard to do because the burden of proof is so heavily weighted against the state.

In addition to the curriculum battles "parental rights" laws would cause, proponents have admitted that these laws could be the first step to obtaining vouchers for religious education. If a parent's right to control the education of a child is absolute, it could be argued that the state must be compelled to provide vouchers because educating one's child in a religious school is the will of the parent.

Proponents of "parental rights" object to the UN Convention on the Rights of Children. They see it as state interference with the family. In a perfect world, every parent would be wise, kind and all-knowing, and every child would be wanted, loved and nurtured. However, we do not live in a perfect world. Old systems of lines of authority may have seemed to have worked, but in reality, whenever any human beings, regardless of age, are treated as property, the potential for abuse greatly increases. The nations of the world have recognized that even children must enjoy basic, fundamental civil rights in order to progress toward realizing justice for all people. This is a development in thinking that we must celebrate rather than attempt to legislate out of existence.

I believe that as a parent I am doing the best job I possibly can. I don't feel threatened by my children discovering ideas that are different from my own. I usually view them as "teaching moments," and they give me a chance to sit down with my kids and discuss why it is I hold certain beliefs while others may have a different opinion. I let my children know that if they need an ear to listen, even if I don't like what I hear, I am available and I will be fair.

I have been the victim of abuse and I have seen parents abusing their children. There's no good excuse for that: it must be stopped. I don't agree with the idea that children "belong" to their parents. As far as I'm concerned, my children belong to God, and I'm just the lucky caretaker.

For these reasons and for my children, I will work to defeat "parental rights" legislation.

> "Since mothers and their children can plunge into poverty after a divorce or separation, improved collection of support payments is essential."

FEDERAL CHILD SUPPORT LAWS BENEFIT CHILDREN

Andrew Cherlin

Andrew Cherlin is a professor of public policy at Johns Hopkins University in Baltimore, Maryland. In the following viewpoint, Cherlin maintains that efforts by state governments to enforce child support are inefficient; therefore, he argues, the federal government should play a larger role in the collection of child support payments. Cherlin advocates the creation of a federal clearinghouse to help employees and states identify delinquent parents and collect payments from them. He insists that such a system could prevent women and children from falling into poverty following divorce. A system similar to the one described by Cherlin was established as part of the welfare reform bill passed in August 1996.

As you read, consider the following questions:

1. According to the author, how many single mothers received the full amount of child support they were due in 1989? How many received partial payment?
2. How does the state-by-state enforcement system impose an undue burden on employers, in Cherlin's opinion?
3. How does the author address the concern that his proposal may infringe upon employees' right to privacy?

From Andrew Cherlin, "Making Deadbeats Pay Up at Work," New York Times, December 30, 1993. Copyright ©1993 by The New York Times Company. Reprinted by permission.

W hat if every father knew he would have to support his children after the breakup of a marital, live-in or even casual relationship?

On January 1, 1994, when an overlooked Federal law went into effect, the United States began answering that question. The law—a delayed provision of the 1988 Family Support Act—requires that, when a court orders a parent to pay child support, the parent's employer must withhold the money from his or her paycheck.

Since mothers and their children can plunge into poverty after a divorce or separation, improved collection of support payments is essential. But although the law is a major advance, it has flaws—in particular, a requirement that each state develop its own system for collecting and distributing support payments.

The sorry story of child support payments is well known. Half of all single mothers were supposed to receive child support in 1989, according to a Census Bureau study. Of those only half received the full amount due that year; one-fourth received partial payment and one-fourth received nothing at all.

The new law is not retroactive; it applies only to divorce or paternity cases resolved after January 1, 1994. Moreover, it allows couples to opt out of the system if they agree on another arrangement or if a judge finds "good cause."

A PATCHWORK SYSTEM

Most troubling, however, is the patchwork state-by-state system of enforcement. Separate state systems are fine if parents who owe support remain in the same state as their ex-partners. Unfortunately, many don't. In the Census Bureau study, 27 percent of mothers who were supposed to receive support, reported that their ex-partners lived out of state. Of that number, 34 percent received nothing in 1989, as against 19 percent of mothers in same-state cases. The 50 separate systems will provide mothers with little help.

And the lack of coordination among the states imposes an unnecessary burden on employers. If I owned a business in New York City and had employees whose ex-partners lived throughout the region, I would quickly drown in paper.

According to New Jersey law, withheld wages go to county probation offices. According to Connecticut law, which will probably change, withheld wages of some employees go to a state agency and the rest directly to the ex-partners. New York may legislate yet a different procedure. If my employees quit, I'm supposed to inform the probation offices, the agencies, the mothers or whomever New York designates.

In a society where half of all children spend time in a single-parent family, this crazy-quilt structure won't adequately protect children against poverty. A Federal clearinghouse is needed to collect and distribute all withheld wages.

Use the IRS

Moving child support collection to the Internal Revenue Service (IRS) would solve some of the most serious problems of the current system. It would allow the vast majority of child support to be collected through income withholding, just as taxes are now paid through withholding.

Paula Roberts, CQ Researcher, January 13, 1995.

Employers would be required to send the names and Social Security numbers of all new employees to the clearinghouse, which would check them against a master list of individuals who owed support. That way collections could be continued easily when parents moved across state lines. And employers could write just one check for the entire amount they withheld.

Some might object that this clearinghouse would add more bureaucracy and infringe upon employee privacy. But we already collect Social Security taxes in a similar way. If we're willing to accept such a system to insure the well-being of the elderly, shouldn't we be willing to do the same for our children?

> "Uncollected child support is a problem. Unfortunately, plans ... to solve it probably won't give children without fathers the sort of help they really need."

FEDERAL CHILD SUPPORT LAWS ARE INEFFECTIVE

Brian Doherty

In the following viewpoint, Brian Doherty opposes an increased federal role in the enforcement of child support. He argues that federal efforts to collect payments from fathers who are delinquent in paying child support are ineffective and result in excessive government control over people's lives. Rather than creating additional government programs in an attempt to obtain payments from "deadbeat dads," according to Doherty, society should pressure fathers to fulfill their moral responsibility to provide for their children. Doherty is an assistant editor for *Reason*, a monthly libertarian magazine.

As you read, consider the following questions:
1. How much did the number of fatherless children increase between 1979 and 1990, according to Doherty?
2. Why are figures on child support payments unreliable, according to the author?
3. In the opinion of David Blankenhorn, who is quoted by the author, why are fathers more important than cash?

From Brian Doherty, "Big Daddy," *Reason*, June 1996. Reprinted by permission of *Reason*.

Children, like hard cases, can make bad law. The child at risk is a stark, powerful image that strikes deep, even if we have no children ourselves. Government endeavors in pursuit of security and prosperity for children have a decided P.R. advantage.

One type of at-risk child is becoming more and more common in America: the child living with only one parent. Such children are, as Dan Quayle got in trouble for suggesting, more prone to a variety of troubles, from criminal activity to having kids out of wedlock themselves.

Fortunately for those leading a dramatic crusade against this growing trend, there's a villain to blame: the deadbeat dad. Fathers across the United States are abandoning their families and their financial responsibilities in ever-growing numbers, the story goes, and only the government—more and more only the federal government—has the power to stop them.

The government has been trying. But it just might be hitting a dead end. Its attempts to do better seem more and more a quick skid down a faster road to serfdom than even [British economist] F.A. Hayek envisioned—and some of its efforts seem more inclined toward helping itself than helping children.

THE FEDERALIZATION OF CHILD SUPPORT

The federalization of child support began in 1975, with the passage of Title IV-D of the Social Security Act, which created the federal Child Support Enforcement and Paternity Establishment program. It also required every state to create and manage its own Office of Child Support, for which the federal government would reimburse 66 percent of the expenses. Before that, child support efforts were the states' business, and the problem of children with only one parent was a relatively small one. Back then, the major reason for single-parent families was the death of one parent or, less commonly, divorce.

But despite federal efforts, the problem continued to grow, and a new wrinkle was added: the child who had never lived with his father to begin with. From 1979 to 1990, the number of children living without a father rose from around 7 million to nearly 10 million, and the percentage of those whose mothers had never been married rose from 19 percent to 30 percent. The federal government in 1988 further expanded its reach over child support with the passage of the Family Support Act, which, among other things, required states to use certain mathematical formulas (of the state's own choice) in deciding child support awards, largely eliminating judicial discretion.

The official line is that $21 billion in overdue child support payments is going uncollected. Figures about unpaid child support are not terribly reliable, however, since they are mostly based on unchecked self-reporting by custodial parents. Surveys done in 1991 by a team of researchers from Arizona State University found that even court records about child support often undercount payments, with many absent dads choosing to pay directly to the mother, not through the court. (Fifty-seven percent of child support money in the ASU survey was paid this way.)

Regardless of the actual total, uncollected child support is a problem. Unfortunately, plans in the works to solve it probably won't give children without fathers the sort of help they really need. But those plans do risk unacceptable levels of government control over everyone's lives.

The Feds are now expanding their reach over child support further. Parts of the omnibus welfare bill [signed by Bill Clinton in August 1996] would enforce on all the states a Uniform Interstate Family Support Act (already adopted by some states). This act modifies the current system controlling interstate child support cases and simplifies the process by ensuring that only one child support order can exist at any time, regardless of where either custodial or noncustodial parent moves.

The bill would also require license revocation—both drivers and professional licenses—for anyone more than 90 days late with a child support payment (some states have such programs already), and create mandatory federal wage withholding and W-4 tracking. Employers would have to report every new hire to a state data bank, which would check the person against a data bank of those with outstanding child support orders; if such an order existed, the employer would have to withhold money from the person's paycheck and forward that money to a state disbursement office. . . .

BEGETTING A LEVIATHAN

A grand example of how the simple acceptance of government responsibility for solving the problems of deadbeat dads can beget a government leviathan is in a 1994 document from the state of Vermont's Office of Child Support on "Recommendations for Improving Child Support in Vermont." Vermont's OCS is kind and understanding—officials acknowledge that inability to pay child support often stems from some sort of substance abuse problem. Thus, "The Office of Child Support is working with the Office of Alcohol and Drug Abuse Programs . . . to develop a model protocol that will 1) identify parents who are not contributing because of substance abuse problems and 2) allow the Office of Child Support and the Family Court to make appropriate referrals for evaluation and perhaps treatment." Other mental health issues can be taken care of the same way, as they too can hinder one's ability to pay child support.

Of course many deadbeat dads really can't afford to pay—the General Accounting Office (GAO) in 1992 estimated possibly as many as 66 percent. So Vermont needs to provide training and job opportunities for those dads—and "Family Court judges and magistrates should, in appropriate cases, make participation in work search or educational programs a requirement that will be enforced by the courts."

THE NUMBER OF CHILDREN IN TWO-PARENT VS. MOTHER-ONLY HOUSEHOLDS

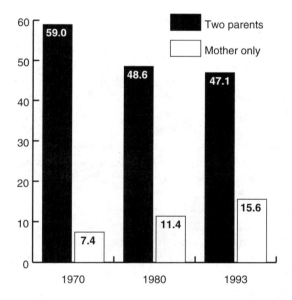

Source: "Marital Status and Living Arrangements: March 1993," Bureau of the Census, 1994.

And since this part of the plan requires a healthy economy in general, the state Department of Economic Development needs to be an integral part of the whole scheme. Also, the privileges the state extends, such as licenses that allow someone to work in a certain profession or drive a car, must be withdrawn from deadbeats. So the state needs a more efficient computer system to crosscheck lists of deadbeats with lists of license holders or applicants. And all employers must report all new hires immediately to a state agency so they can find out if they've just hired a deadbeat from whose paycheck they'll have to withdraw money. And since deadbeats can cross state lines, all of these ideas ought to be implemented in a coordinated way nationwide.

It all makes perfect sense—and it all essentially makes anyone in the grip of the child support system a total ward of the state. It also enmeshes anyone foolish enough to hire that person, and creates apparatuses of surveillance and control that could easily be extended to other purposes less clearly noble than mulcting cash from deadbeat dads.

But it's all for the children, right?

David Blankenhorn, author of the book *Fatherless America*, wonders if our current child support system really is good for kids.

"The only way to get money," he concludes, "is to have men who believe they want to be fathers. No child support program will work when the demographic trends [of more and more fatherless children] are going in the opposite direction."

Blankenhorn argues at length in his book that merely squeezing cash out of fathers isn't good enough. Fathers are more important than just cash; growing up without a father's presence is worse than growing up without a father's bucks. The pathologies of fatherless children are caused by lack of a father's care, guidance, and image, not just his money. The only solution, a "sober" and "pessimistic" Blankenhorn says, is to reemphasize "the moral responsibility for a man to support his child, to constantly remind them they are doing something shameful and unmanly" if they don't. . . .

Despite all the money the federal government is spending . . . the child support bureaucracy still isn't running efficiently even on its own terms. A recent GAO report goes on for dozens of pages about the child support bureaucracies' administrative problems, and the insistence that a larger, more intrusive bureaucracy is needed indicates that they aren't bringing the problem under control. Government can almost never admit that some problems are simply intractable in a free society. As long as people continue to choose to have children out of wedlock—the result of social and moral changes the government is powerless to halt, except on the margins through changes in welfare policy—we will continue to have men who father children but do not feel like, or are made not to feel like, fathers.

So long as they don't feel responsible, tinkering with changes in government programs won't make them so. "I could imagine a society in which [current crackdown efforts] would work," says Blankenhorn. "But it would need to be an authoritarian state."

PERIODICAL BIBLIOGRAPHY

The following articles have been selected to supplement the diverse views presented in this chapter. Addresses are provided for periodicals not indexed in the *Readers' Guide to Periodical Literature*, the *Alternative Press Index*, the *Social Sciences Index*, or the *Index to Legal Periodicals and Books*.

America	"Hungrier in America," May 18, 1996.
Ellen L. Bassuk, Angela Browne, and John C. Buckner	"Single Mothers and Welfare," *Scientific American*, October 1996.
Nina Bernstein	"Are Welfare Cuts a Foster Care Burden?" *New York Times*, November 19, 1995.
T. Berry Brazelton	"My Dream for America's Children," *Family Circle*, May 16, 1995. Available from 110 Fifth Ave., New York, NY 10011.
Children Today	"Shalala Calls for a New Era of Support to Families with Infants and Toddlers," Summer/Fall 1995.
Christian Century	"U.S. Lax on Hunger," November 6, 1996.
Hillary Rodham Clinton	"There Is No Such Thing as 'Other People's' Children," *Los Angeles Times*, March 14, 1995. Available from Times Mirror Square, Los Angeles, CA 90053.
Lynn Crandall	"Hope for the Children," *Family Circle*, November 1, 1996.
Jeffrey L. Katz	"Welfare Overhaul Law," *Congressional Quarterly Weekly Report*, September 21, 1996.
National Catholic Reporter	"Republican Revolution Leaves a World of Hunger," November 10, 1995. Available from PO Box 281, Kansas City, MO 64141.
Paul Offner	"Kid Stuff: How Deadbeat Dads Can Reform Welfare," *New Republic*, August 1, 1994.
Paul Offner	"Welfare Dads: A Better Solution to the Welfare Mess," *New Republic*, February 13, 1995.
Katha Pollitt	"Subject to Debate," *Nation*, February 13, 1995.
Howard G. Schneiderman	"Antisocial Personalities, Antidemocratic Solutions," *Society*, November/December 1996.
Donna Shalala	"Meeting the Needs of Young Children," *Children Today*, Summer/Fall 1994.
Thomas Sowell	"Children As Footballs: The Welfare of Children Is Being Sacrificed to Politics and to the Resentment of Adults," *Forbes*, January 16, 1995.

CHAPTER 3

HOW CAN NEEDY CHILDREN BEST BE HELPED?

CHAPTER PREFACE

Pamela's story is typical of many needy children. She was born addicted to crack cocaine. Her parents were not married. Her father was a heroin addict and her mother, Veronica, was a crack addict who already had two illegitimate children fathered by different men. Pamela's parents and older sister, Nyjah, were living in a broken-down rusting car at the time of Pamela's birth. Poverty and drugs marked the child's early life.

Fortunately for Pamela, her mother wanted to change their lives. Shortly after Pamela's birth, Veronica graduated from a drug rehabilitation program and found subsidized housing; later she moved into a shelter with her three children.

Veronica's drug treatment and housing were both subsidized by the federal government. During times when she could not care for her children, they were taken in by foster parents, who were subsidized by the state government. Although Veronica completed a computer-programming course, she could not find a job, and she still receives government support. However, her children are healthy and cared for and are being educated.

The drug addiction, illegitimacy, homelessness, and poverty that have marked Pamela's life are common among the needy children of America. Are the government programs utilized by her mother the best way to help such needy children? Some experts say yes and point to Pamela and others as evidence that such policies work. Investigative journalist and former welfare recipient Rita Henley Jensen argues that many single women need government welfare programs in order to care for their children and improve their lives. She insists that welfare was the key that enabled her to gain an education and raise her two children on her own.

Others, however, argue that if Pamela's mother had never had any public assistance, she might not have had any illegitimate children in the first place. Conservatives William Bennett, Jack Kemp, and Vin Weber, for example, maintain that "welfare is illegitimacy's economic lifeline"—that is, if women know there will be no one, including the government, to support them and their illegitimate children, they will be far more careful to avoid having children they cannot care for.

There are many suggestions concerning how to help America's neediest children. Some involve government programs while others require the participation of individuals and private organizations. In the following chapter, the authors discuss the effectiveness of some of these measures.

"Some—if not many—orphanages
in this country appear to have
known how to break the cycles of
poverty, neglect, and abuse for hordes
of children."

NEEDY CHILDREN CAN THRIVE IN ORPHANAGES

Richard B. McKenzie

A century ago, many children who were abandoned or whose
parents died were raised in orphanages. These "homes" became
notorious for their poor conditions, and public support for orphanages declined. In recent years, though, several politicians
have suggested that orphanages could provide a better home life
for many parentless children than the current foster care system
does. In the following viewpoint, Richard B. McKenzie echoes
this view. He cites a study that followed the progress of the children of three orphanages. As adults, McKenzie reports, these individuals did as well as or better than average Americans in their
economic, social, and personal achievements. McKenzie is Walter B. Gerken Professor of Enterprise and Society at the Graduate
School of Management of the University of California, Irvine,
and the author of The Home: A Memoir of Growing Up in an Orphanage.

As you read, consider the following questions:

1. How did the educational achievements of the orphanage
   alumni differ from those of the general public, according to
   McKenzie?
2. How did the orphanage alumni differ from the general
   public in their attitudes toward life, according to the author?
3. What questions should child-care researchers ask, in
   McKenzie's opinion?

From Richard B. McKenzie, "Orphanages: The Real Story." Reprinted with permission of
the author and the Public Interest, no. 123, Spring 1996, pp. 100-104; ©1996 by National
Affairs, Inc.

When the word "orphanage" is used, Americans typically cringe, imagining that the children who grew up in one had the crudest and cruelest of childhoods. Harsh, unrelenting critics of orphanages continue to play on these popular images of orphanages, but few researchers have thought to ask former orphans for their assessments of their childhood experiences. And no one to date has sought to assess the long-term impact of orphanages on the lives and well-being of the children who grew up in them.

To correct this deficiency in the ongoing welfare-reform debate, the preliminary findings from a survey of the alumni from three orphanages—a Jewish home in the Midwest, a Presbyterian home in the South, and a non-sectarian home in the Midwest—are reported. The people who were in the homes, all of whom are now 44 years of age and older, were asked to report what they have accomplished over their lives and to assess the value of their childhood experiences in their respective institutions.

ORPHANAGE ALUMNI FARE BETTER

Generally speaking, the alumni have surpassed, by wide margins, their counterparts in the general population on a variety of social and economic measures. The findings from this study stand in sharp contrast to the claims of many child-care experts and policy commentators regarding the impact of orphanages on the children.

The findings reported here were gathered from surveying the alumni of three homes that served mainly disadvantaged (as distinguished from severely troubled) children. The non-sectarian home, which had a 100-acre campus in rural Ohio, operated from revenues received primarily from a single benefactor. The Presbyterian home, which had 1,500 acres of land in rural North Carolina, received most of its funding from foundations, individuals, and the Presbyterian church. The Jewish home, which once operated on a 20-acre urban campus in Ohio and then on a 28-acre campus in a smaller town, also received most of its funding from private, mainly religious-based, contributions. All three homes have since changed their mission to serve only severely troubled children.

A survey, extending over eight pages, was mailed in the spring of 1995 to the more than 1,200 alumni on the mailing lists of the homes' alumni associations (which includes the names of residents before and after the change in the mid-1940s). Only the surveys from people who were at the homes before their change in missions were included in the computation of the summary statistics provided below. A total of more than 600 questionnaires from the targeted alumni were returned, which suggests a response rate for the targeted group of more than 50 percent.

The average year of the respondents' arrival at their respective homes was 1933. The alumni were, on average, eight years old when they arrived at their homes, and they stayed for an average of eight years (with most staying until they graduated from high school). The respondents, who are all white, are fairly evenly divided between males (52 percent) and females (48 percent). The alumni's average age today is 69 (the youngest respondent is 44 and the oldest is 96).

MEASURING SUCCESS

If the claims of child-care professionals, many of whom assert that orphanages only damaged the children in their charge, are true, then we might expect the alumni of homes for children, as a group, to have done poorly (or, at least, not well) on a variety of social and economic measures. However, a preliminary examination of the responses from the alumni of these three homes reveals the exact opposite:

Education. The alumni, 44 years of age and older, surpassed the general white population, 40 years of age and older, at every rung of the educational ladder, except at the high-school level at which both groups had practically identical graduation rates, 81 percent and 80 percent, respectively. However, while fewer than 22 percent of white Americans 40 and older had college degrees in 1993, more than 24 percent of the orphans had such degrees, a difference of 9 percent. Less than 9 percent of white Americans 40 and older had advanced degrees. Nearly 12 percent of the orphans had advanced degrees, a difference of 33 percent.

Unemployment. The unemployment rate for the country's entire labor force was over 6 percent in 1995. The alumni who were not retired had an unemployment rate of 1 percent.

Household income. The orphans 44 to 54 years of age had a median income 16 percent higher than their counterparts in the general white population. The orphans 55 to 64 had a median income 32 percent higher than their counterparts, and the orphans 65 and older had a median household income 75 percent higher than their counterparts.

Poverty. In 1992, . . . the national poverty rate was close to 15 percent for Americans of all races and 12 percent for all white Americans. The national poverty rate for white Americans in age groups 45 and older was between 5 percent and 6 percent. The poverty rate of the respondents was no higher than 3 percent.

Public assistance. Less than 3 percent of the orphans have ever been on any form of public assistance (not counting Social Security). In 1992 alone, 19 percent of the general population received at least one form of public assistance (not counting Social Security).

Time in prison. A white American has a 1.6 percent chance of spending some time in a *state* prison during his or her life. Less than 1 percent of the alumni report ever spending any time in a jail, state prison, or federal prison (suggesting a lower rate of incarceration than the general population).

EMOTIONAL HEALTH AND HAPPINESS

Emotional disorders. Between 20 percent and 28 percent of all Americans at any point in time suffer from some form of diagnosable psychiatric or addictive disorder. Only 13 percent of the orphans report ever suffering from a mental or emotional disorder sufficiently serious to have warranted, at any time in their lives, the help of a psychologist or psychiatrist, and less than one-fifth of those former orphans who reported such problems (2 percent of all respondents) felt their problems were related, in any way, to their experiences at their homes for children.

Voter participation. About 76 percent of Americans who were 45 years old and older voted in the 1992 election. Nearly 88 percent of the former orphans voted, an 11 percent higher turnout rate (with the split in their votes for president more or less mirroring the election results).

Attitude toward life. The following question has been posed in a variety of public-opinion polls to a large number of Americans practically every year since 1957: "Taking all things together, how would you say things are going these days?" In 1994, 29 percent of the respondents in the general population indicated they were "very happy"; 59 percent indicated they were "somewhat happy"; and 12 percent indicated they were "not too happy." The former orphans, on the other hand, indicate a far more positive attitude toward life: 58 percent were "very happy" (exactly twice the percentage for the general population); 37 percent were "somewhat happy"; and 5 percent were "not too happy" (less than half the percentage for the general population).

Preference for institutional care. The orphans appear to have an overwhelming preference for their way of growing up over the next best alternative. When asked if they preferred to grow up in their orphanages or foster care, just over 92 percent preferred their orphanages, less than 2 percent preferred foster care, and 6 percent reported not knowing enough to say one way or the other. When asked if they preferred to grow up in their orphanages or with the available members of their own families, 75 percent of the respondents chose their orphanages, whereas less than 16 percent chose their own families, with less than 10 percent not being able to say.

QUALITY RESIDENTIAL CARE

It would be nice to live in a world where all children had loving, caring families, one in which there weren't hundreds of thousands of kids whose families irretrievably were broken because of drugs, alcohol, and abuse. It would be great if family preservation programs could put all families back together. Such a world doesn't exist, however. . . .

Some people see only two options: a healthy, healing family or a dehumanizing "institution." However, there is a middle ground—quality residential care. I probably would not have believed this myself if I were not associated with Boys Town or did not know of so many other good residential facilities across America.

Many opponents of institutions have visited Boys Town and gone away saying, "I did not think it could be done." Not only has it been accomplished in the family-style homes of Boys Town, these successful programs have been replicated in 14 major metropolitan areas across America. Other agencies have gone down the same road of success.

Val J. Peter (executive director of Boys Town), *USA Today*, November 1995.

Cost of care. Although the orphans had advantages other children did not have (for example, some former orphans reported having access to recreational facilities and the fine arts), the former orphans were not reared in the lap of high-priced care. The cost of care (covering housing, recreation, supervision, and basic amenities) per child around 1950 for the alumni from the Presbyterian home was less than $3,000 per year—in 1995 dollars! (When the cost of education and administration are added, the per child cost reached no higher than $5,000 a year—again, in 1995 dollars.)

UNDERMINING THE CRITICISM

Clearly, this survey of former orphans has limitations, the most important of which is that the respondents were not drawn randomly from the national population of all former orphans. The alumni who had good experiences might be more likely to be on the alumni mailing lists and more likely to respond. Tracking down all former residents of any given home for children, and then surveying all or just a random sample of them, is simply not possible.

However, even after allowing for some upward bias, the results do seriously undermine some of the critics' most sweeping, if not reckless, negative assessments applied to all orphanages. The findings also strongly indicate that, while institutional care may not be desirable for *all* disadvantaged children, it was helpful for many. The study strongly suggests that at least *some*—if not many—orphanages in this country appear to have known how to break the cycles of poverty, neglect, and abuse for hordes of children, and they did it, often with much gratitude from a majority of the alumni.

The evidence also suggests that partisans in the child-care debate would be well advised to revisit some strategically important questions, not the least of which are: What types of homes were successful? Did not homes for children have a higher ratio of successes to failures than the current foster-care system? To what extent can the attributes of the successful homes of yesterday be duplicated today?

"The historical evidence of the past century strongly highlights that orphanages did not solve the plight of poor families."

NEEDY CHILDREN CANNOT THRIVE IN ORPHANAGES

Megan E. McLaughlin

Megan E. McLaughlin is executive director and chief executive officer of the Federation of Protestant Welfare Agencies, an umbrella organization of volunteer human service agencies serving New York City. In the following viewpoint, McLaughlin opposes the proposal to revive orphanages as a solution for needy children. She contends that orphanages are cold, unfriendly institutions that cannot provide the nurturing care children need. Rather than placing children in orphanages, McLaughlin argues, society should focus on cultivating strong, healthy families, which she says are the best environment for raising children.

As you read, consider the following questions:

1. What assumptions about poor parents do supporters of orphanages make, according to the author?
2. What were the conditions found in the orphanages of the nineteenth century, as described by McLaughlin?
3. How do orphanages compare in cost to other programs aimed at helping the poor, according to the author?

Excerpted from Megan E. McLaughlin, "Orphanages Are Not the Solution," *USA Today* magazine, November 1995. Reprinted by permission of the Society for the Advancement of Education, ©1995.

In 1994, during the early days of the public debate on welfare reform, Speaker of the House Newt Gingrich ignited a media firestorm by suggesting that orphanages are better for poor children than life with a mother on Aid to Families with Dependent Children (AFDC). Responding to blistering criticism, he first defended the proposal by invoking the idyllic orphanage life of the 1938 film *Boys Town*, finally retreating, at least rhetorically, from the entire controversy. Orphanages became just another blip on the nation's radar screen, or so it seemed.

In fact, the plan to revive orphanages was embedded in the Personal Responsibility Act, the Republican plan for welfare reform [defeated in January 1996], and was a major piece of the Republican Contract With America. The Republicans' pledge promised to balance the budget, protect defense spending, and cut taxes, targeting programs for the poor—cash assistance, food, housing, medical, and child care—as the big areas for major budget savings. Parents who are poor, it has been predicted, would have little or no choice but to watch their children board the orphan trains in search of shelter and food. The political question remains: Are orphanages the solution—or part of the solution—to the welfare problem?

THE RISE AND FALL OF ORPHANAGES

Orphanages for poor children are not a new proposal. They originated in England in the 17th century and were adopted in the U.S. in the early 18th century out of concerns and biases similar to those driving current proposals. Though the word "orphan" is defined as "a child deprived of parents," American orphanages always have housed youngsters who had parents—usually poor mothers—as well as those who did not.

Earlier in 17th-century America, even though no child welfare system existed, orphans as well as children of the poor were presumed to require attention from the public authorities. The care of poor children has been a recurring theme and concern in this country. The assumptions of those early years continue to prevail today. If mothers and fathers cannot provide adequately for their kids, they are assumed to be inadequate parents; are perceived as bad role models because they do not work, and their children should be saved from them; should be stigmatized and made social outcasts; and should lose their right to plan for their offspring. . . .

When poor mothers could not provide for their offspring in the 18th and 19th centuries, society solved their "poverty" problem by opening orphanages. As the human and economic costs became starkly apparent, other alternatives were sought.

By the 20th century, the use of orphanages declined dramatically. Child welfare workers began focusing on strengthening families as the best way to rear youngsters. The 1909 White House Conference on Children declared that "homelife is the highest and finest product of civilization" and stressed the superiority of families over institutional care. The new focus on families led to an increase in the use of foster homes, and orphanages began to transform themselves into "residential treatment centers," with smaller facilities, professional staff, and even higher costs.

BIG GOVERNMENT INTERFERENCE

I disagree with those who suggest that children should be taken from their parents and put in orphanages solely because they were born out of wedlock and their parents are poor. This is big government interference into the lives of private citizens at its worst.

Hillary Rodham Clinton, *Newsweek*, January 16, 1995.

Over the next 70 years, the use of orphanages declined, first in ideology, then gradually in practice. This process was helped along by the passage, in 1935, of the Aid to Dependent Children (ADC) program, a small part of President Franklin D. Roosevelt's Social Security Act. This legislation supported the idea of poor mothers caring for their own offspring in their homes instead of institutionalizing them. This was achieved by providing needy single-parent families with a small monthly stipend.

With this new thrust on strengthening families, the percentage of kids in institutions dropped from 57.8% in 1933 to 31% in 1962 and 17.1% in 1989. In 1980, the Adoption Assistance Act further reduced use of institutional care by encouraging the return of children to their biological parents and putting an emphasis on services to prevent out-of-home placement.

DANGEROUS AND REGRESSIVE

Today, Republicans are choosing to return to failed options by reinstating the dangerous and regressive system of the 19th century. An analysis of the Personal Responsibility Act reveals that it embodied and exemplified the very assumptions that existed then. These assumptions are given further credibility by conservative apostles who provide unfounded rationales for these policies. Gingrich claims his own inspiration comes from former drug czar William Bennett's 1990 suggestion that children of drug users be placed in orphanages. Conservative author Charles Murray argues that all AFDC spending should be redirected to the construction of orphanages for poor women's offspring. He reinforces his proposal in his best-selling book, The Bell Curve, which claims, among other things, that African-Americans are genetically inferior. A pseudoscientific finding contends to validate the common perception that the majority of those on welfare are black and/or Hispanic, then exploits existing and pervasive racial divisions. This, in turn, makes it easier to justify the idea of orphanages for AFDC children. [AFDC was replaced by a state-centered welfare system in August 1996.]

There are those who would characterize this statement as gross exaggeration. While they prefer to ignore the racism that is embedded in many of the proposals for welfare reform, they need only familiarize themselves with the statements made by Republican Joseph Bruno, Majority Leader of the New York State Senate. Bruno publicly accused State Assembly Speaker Sheldon Silver of not wanting to discuss welfare reform because he "is beholden to blacks and Hispanics . . . the people that got their hands out."

The reintroduction of orphanages into the political discourse as the preferred system for caring for kids with poor parents is consistent with the trend toward increased institutionalization. This is exemplified by the "three strikes and you're in" proposals for convicted felons and the growing support for treating children as criminals at younger and younger ages. However, the U.S. tried institutionalization of children in the past, using orphanages in particular, and they failed miserably.

OVERCROWDED AND HAZARDOUS

The orphanages of the 19th century were overcrowded and hazardous to the physical health of children. In the 1850s, the Philadelphia House of Refuge crammed 100 children into five dormitories; in Charleston, South Carolina, 200 children slept in 10 rooms; and in the New York House of Refuge, bathtubs held 15 or 20 boys at a time. Photographs reveal the overcrowding and poor health conditions that were rampant. As recently as the 1980s, audits of New York City's congregate care facilities uncovered serious defects in health and safety. Hazards included disease, repeated violations of fire codes, and injuries to children from broken furniture and scalding tap water. Clearly, in the past, life in orphanages greatly increased the number of youngsters condemned to abusive living situations and, more tragically, at great risk of abuse. Recent studies have found that the rate of abuse and neglect in institutions is more than twice that in foster homes.

It has been demonstrated that orphanages are harmful and have a deleterious impact on many children, especially those who are under six years old. (More than 5,700,000 kids under the age of six are poor.) It also is known that separation from parents can cause extreme trauma. Psychological studies continue to hold that the summary removal of youngsters from parents who have been major caregivers poses a severe threat to their development and should be allowed only under conditions in which physical survival is at stake.

Although the trauma of being removed from one's family and placed in an orphanage can be overcome by later exposure to a loving and stimulating environment, numerous studies reveal that orphanages usually do not provide such an environment. Instead, children tend to confront bleak, impersonal surroundings and have adult contact only with overworked staff members who cannot give them the attention they need. Under these circumstances, it is no wonder that those who left orphanages after long stays show severe deficits in development, have trouble forming and maintaining close relationships, and have difficulty with conceptual thinking, increased tendencies towards unacceptable social behavior, and poor impulse control.

ORPHANAGES ARE EXPENSIVE

Orphanages not only will harm children, they also will affect taxpayers. They are extremely costly, as even supporters of drastic welfare changes acknowledge. In contrast, AFDC consumes just one cent out of every Federal tax dollar. Elimination of the entire program would not have a major impact on the Federal budget or the deficit. In fact, the increased use of orphanages would boost over-all governmental spending, as well as bureaucratic control over the lives of poor families and poor children.

Estimates of the savings from the proposed changes and reductions in the welfare reform proposal would not be sufficient to cover the costs of orphanages. In New York State, the U.S. Department of Health and Human Services estimates that, of the 741,000 children on AFDC, 349,000 would be denied benefits, saving $27,116,000. This amount would pay for a mere 743 orphanage slots.

The projections are similar for other states. In California, more than 1,000,000 kids would lose benefits, and the Federal savings of $64,152,000 would be adequate to pay for just

1,758 orphanage slots. Even if one in five youngsters ends up in orphanages, the total outlay would be $36,500,000,000 per year. The bases for these projections are not exaggerated; if anything, they are underestimated. They assume that states will not adopt more restrictive options and are based on an average yearly cost of $36,500 per child. At Chicago's Mercy Home, the cost is $59,500 per child per year; at Boys Town, $47,000. Furthermore, these figures do not include the capital and start up expenses that would be necessary for there to be creation of new orphanages. . . .

STRENGTHENING THE FAMILY

The historical evidence of the past century strongly highlights that orphanages did not solve the plight of poor families in the past and will not do so today. It also underscores the need for policies that strengthen, rather than break up, families. The family is society's most fundamental institution. Nationally, there is widespread consensus that children thrive best in families and, thus, that it is necessary to support families.

As the U.S. approaches the 21st century, the political question is: How is this to be done? Should orphanages be created to institutionalize youngsters whose mothers are too poor to support them? Or should society create jobs, strengthen education, and provide child care to enable mothers and fathers to earn enough to provide for their families?

Even though the future depends on the strength of families' health and the well-being of children, the nation seems unable to act on such knowledge and beliefs. Strong families only can be ensured if parents are provided with the means to earn a living at adequate wages; have access to quality child care, training, and education; and, in times of crisis, can count on the support of a safety net. We know what must be done and need the courage to fight for this vision. The question remains: Do we have the will?

"Parents usually develop warm and
secure relationships with their
adopted infants."

CHILDREN CAN THRIVE IN ADOPTED FAMILIES

Bruce Bower

For years studies have found that adopted children have more
emotional and behavioral problems than their nonadopted
peers. In the following viewpoint, Bruce Bower argues that
more recent research has produced much different results. According to Bower, these new studies show that children adopted
as infants usually bond with their adoptive parents, develop positive self-images, and experience good mental health. Bower is
the behavioral sciences editor for *Science News*.

As you read, consider the following questions:
1. What positive characteristics do adoptive parents share,
   according to Bower?
2. How well do children involved in interracial adoptions
   adjust, according to the author?
3. What were the results of the study of adoptees conducted by
   Michael Bohman, as summarized by the author?

From Bruce Bower, "Adapting to Adoption," *Science News*, vol. 146, no. 7, August 13,
1994, pp. 104-106. Reprinted with permission.

W elcome to the adoptive family, where home life takes on a decidedly different look depending on whether it is refracted through the lens of mental health clinicians or behavioral researchers.

For more than 40 years, psychiatrists and others who treat emotional and behavioral problems have noted that adopted children and teenagers make up a disproportionate number of their patients. About 2 percent of children under age 18 in the United States are adopted by unrelated parents, but they make up 5 percent of children in psychotherapy, 10 to 15 percent of youngsters in residential treatment and psychiatric hospitals, and 6 to 9 percent of those identified in schools as suffering from various learning disabilities. An estimated 1 million children in the United States now live with adoptive parents.

Clinicians have focused on the roadblocks to an adoptee's healthy development. According to various mental health workers, adoptive parents and kids often struggle to form strong emotional bonds. The parents tend to ruminate about a child's biological parents; the children begin to realize at age 5 to 7 that one set of parents rejected them and to struggle with a sense of loss and bewilderment about their biological roots. Their self-esteem drops; they cannot seem to make close friends. Adolescent adoptees show a propensity for delinquency, depression, and a confused self-image.

Search movement advocates, who lobby for giving adoptees access to their adoption records so they can seek out their biological parents, take this position further. Adopted people need information about their genetic origins in order to feel whole and secure, they argue; those who lack this knowledge stumble through life feeling isolated and incomplete. Some in the search movement press for the elimination of adoption.

Yet in the past decade, a growing body of research on adoptees who do not receive psychological help indicates that parents usually develop warm and secure relationships with their adopted infants, whose emotional health and self-image throughout the school years equal those of children living with biological parents. Rates of psychological and behavioral problems rise in youngsters adopted after infancy, probably due largely to neglect, abuse, and multiple changes in caretakers before adoption, according to these investigators.

Organizations representing adoptive families consider such findings a refreshing antidote to the clinical emphasis on adoption's inherent problems and to the widespread unease about parents raising children conceived by others, especially children who come from different races or nations.

"This issue is a tangled ball of yarn, and adoption research is only in its infancy," asserts Anu R. Sharma, a psychologist at the Search Institute, a Minneapolis based organization that studies children and teenagers.

"Useful guidelines for adoptive parents are in short supply, while the adoption process itself has become more diverse," adds Steven L. Nickman, a psychiatrist at Massachusetts General Hospital in Boston. "Adoption is a highly political issue."

Consider interracial adoption. In 1972, the National Association of Black Social Workers branded the adoption of black children by white parents "cultural genocide," a position it still holds. Most adoption agencies try to place children with same-race parents and avoid interracial matches. About 500 black children get adopted by whites annually.

In the case of the approximately 10,000 children adopted annually from abroad by U.S. residents, officials in their countries of origin often confront home-grown pressures to bar this practice.

Some countries allow international adoptions for a short time, then suddenly withhold children from foreigners, as happened in Rumania. South Korea, the major source of babies for international adoption over the past 40 years, plans to phase out such placements by 1996.

On the domestic front, an Illinois Supreme Court judge ordered last month that a 3½-month-old boy be taken from his adoptive parents, who had raised him from the age of 4 days, and given to his biological father, who argued that the adoption had occurred without his knowledge or consent. The adoptive parents plan to appeal the ruling to the U.S. Supreme Court. For now, the boy remains with them.

Still, societies around the world allow, and in some cases encourage, the transfer of children to nonbiological parents. Adoption as either a legal or an informal method of incorporating new members into a family extends back to the earliest centers of civilization, including Rome, Greece, India, China, and Babylonia.

Systematic efforts to understand the emotional adjustment of adopted youngsters have emerged only in the past 25 years. The latest study, conducted by the Search Institute and released in June, finds that teenagers adopted as infants generally have positive self-concepts, warm relationships with their parents, and psychological health comparable to that of nonadopted teens.

"This flies in the face of many clinical reports that adopted teenagers have all sorts of problems," contends Anu Sharma, who participated in the project, directed by institute psychologist Peter L. Benson.

With the help of public and private adoption agencies in Colorado, Illinois, Minnesota, and Wisconsin, the researchers recruited 715 families with teenagers who had been adopted as infants. A total of 1,262 parents, 881 adopted adolescents, and 78 nonadopted siblings completed surveys on psychological and family characteristics.

THE PARENT-CHILD BOND

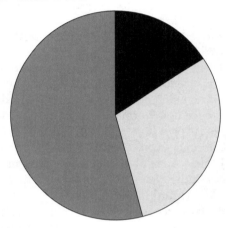

■ 54% Close ties to both parents

□ 30% Deep bond with one parent

■ 16% Lack of strong attachment to either parent

Responses of adopted children to questions concerning the strength of the emotional ties to their adoptive parents.

Source: Bruce Bower, *Science News*, August 13, 1994.

Most adopted teens regarded their adoption as a fact of life that made little difference in how they viewed themselves; about one-quarter reported that adoption loomed large in their self-views. Adopted girls cited more struggles with identity and self-esteem than adopted boys; however, such sex differences prove difficult to interpret because teenage girls find it easier to express their feelings than teenage boys.

Nearly two-thirds of the adopted youngsters noted an interest in meeting their biological parents, mainly to see what they look like, to tell them "I'm happy," or to find out the reasons for their adoptions. At the same time, only 9 percent reported missing or longing for biological parents.

In addition, adopted adolescents cited emotional attachments to their parents as strong as those of their nonadopted siblings. Close ties to both parents emerged for 54 percent; another 30 percent had a deep bond with one parent; 16 percent reported the lack of a strong attachment to either parent.

Nearly all parents—95 percent—said they experienced a strong attachment to their adopted child.

Families displayed considerable skill in communication and discipline, as well as a low rate of parental divorce and separation, perhaps partly reflecting a successful preadoption screening process at most agencies. Parents typically maintained a delicate balance in discussing adoption with their children, neither denying its existence nor overplaying it.

On measures of psychological adjustment, nearly three-quarters of the adopted teens showed good mental health. Measures included tobacco, alcohol, and illicit drug use; sexual activity; depression and suicide attempts; delinquent and violent acts; school problems; and bulimia.

A slightly smaller percentage of good mental health—assessed in a similar survey conducted by the Search Institute since 1990—appears in 51,098 teenagers attending public school in the same four states in which the adoptees live, Benson and Sharma assert. Another research team found a slightly higher proportion of good mental health in a national sample of 1,719 teenagers, studied with a battery of clinical scales in 1989, who had not received mental health services or required special academic help.

Reasons for these small differences remain unclear, although Sharma considers similarities in mental health across the three studies more significant.

One-third of the adopted teens had received counseling or psychotherapy, although most of those reported good mental health. Adoptive parents may seek out such services more willingly than other parents, Sharma notes. Also, parents and teachers may assume that adopted adolescents are more prone to emotional problems and refer them for counseling sooner than they do other teens.

The 289 interracially adopted adolescents in the Search Institute survey—most from Korea—displayed psychological health and identity formation comparable to those of adoptees in same-race families.

Adoptees reported much more involvement in churches and in volunteer and community organizations than comparison groups, notes psychologist Matthew K. McGue of the University of Minnesota in Minneapolis, who is participating in further analyses of the data. This may reflect a particular emphasis on such activities by adoptive parents, he says.

Rumination about biological parents tended to occur in adopted teens who showed the most signs of depression or anxiety, McGue adds. "For them, adoption seems to be one more thing to worry about," he holds.

Despite its intriguing glimpse into the lives of adopted teenagers, the Search Institute project contains some important limitations. Half the adoptive families originally contacted for the survey declined to participate, yielding a nonrandom sample; a nonadopted control group given the same survey was not included; and researchers failed to establish how much security teenagers derived from their reported sense of emotional attachment to adoptive parents.

Moreover, the researchers looked only at parents who worked with agencies that provided education and support after the adoption. It remains unclear whether the findings apply to independent adoptions—now the majority of unrelated domestic adoptions.

Several other studies support the positive cast on adoption provided by the Search Institute survey.

In Sweden, psychiatrist Michael Bohman at the University of Umea directed a longitudinal study of 164 infant adoptees, 208 children raised by biological mothers who had registered them for adoption and then changed their minds, and 203 children placed in foster homes (where many were adopted by age 7).

At age 11, about 20 percent of boys and girls in these three groups exhibited serious emotional and behavioral problems, as rated by their teachers. A much smaller proportion of their classmates got tagged as "problem children."

But at age 15, adopted children rebounded. Teacher ratings of their social, emotional, and academic skills equaled those given their classmates. Youngsters living with biological mothers who reneged on adoption plans and those in foster homes lagged considerably behind the adoptees on these measures.

Infant adoptees continued to do well at ages 18 and 23, but higher rates of alcohol-related problems and criminal behavior, as well as lower scores on intelligence and psychological tests, characterized the other two groups.

Bohman and a colleague describe these findings in The Psychology of Adoption (D. Brodzinsky and M. Schechter, eds. 1990, Oxford University Press).

In the same book, Janet L. Hoopes, a psychologist at Bryn Mawr (Pa.) College, describes a study of 50 adopted and 41 nonadopted teenagers age 15 to 18. All adoptions had occurred by age 2.

Extensive interviews uncovered no differences between the groups on several measures of identity formation, as well as in family and peer relations, school performance, and self-esteem.

The 16 adoptees interested in finding their biological parents showed slightly more difficulty in identity formation, Hoopes says. As a group, "searchers" more often reported unhappy family relationships and perceived themselves as more strikingly mismatched with adoptive parents in physical appearance.

However, adoptees unanimously considered their adoptive parents as among the most significant persons in their lives; none placed his or her biological parents in that category.

A 20-year study of 204 white families with adopted children, most of them black, also documents healthy emotional development. As the youngsters matured, they developed a clear sense of racial identity, says Rita J. Simon, a sociologist at American University in Washington, D.C.

Youngsters in that investigation included 157 interracial adoptees, 42 white adoptees, and 167 biological children of the adopting parents. "Adoptees didn't have worse or different problems than their biological siblings," Simon says.

Around age 11, about one in five adopted children—mainly boys—began stealing money or possessions from family members. But as in the Swedish study, this behavior stopped by age 15 and may have represented a testing of family affection and commitment at a time of increased awareness about the meaning of adoption, Simon contends.

She and Howard Altstein, a social worker at the University of Maryland in Baltimore, describe their project in The Case for Transracial Adoption (1994, American University Press).

Although scientific measures of identity, racial or otherwise, contain much room for improvement, these studies document the overall success of interracial adoptions, holds psychiatrist Ezra E.H. Griffith of Yale University.

Still, political opposition to interracial adoption remains strong, Griffith says. Only Texas forbids a focus on placing children with parents of the same race. Child-welfare workers often hold minority children in foster or institutional care for years rather than place them with white parents. Legislation approved by the U.S. Senate and pending in the House would prohibit delaying or denying adoptions on the basis of race.

Meanwhile, clinicians who treat adoptees and their families agree that this family arrangement generally works well, especially for those adopted as infants. But in their view, the Search Institute survey and related research gloss over the complexities of identity development with which all adoptees must deal. These heighten the risk of psychological problems in late childhood and adolescence.

"As joyous as adoption is, adopted teenagers need to make sense of the more complicated circumstances that led to who they are," contends psychologist Joyce Pavao of the Family Center in Somerville, Mass. "They have to acknowledge and deal with a sense of loss for their biological parents and the issue of physical dissimilarity to adoptive parents and relatives." Pavao regards these as typical concerns and says that clinicians have tended to "pathologize" them.

Serious emotional or identity problems probably occur most often in children adopted after infancy and by parents of a different race, maintains Steven Nickman of Massachusetts General Hospital. Even kids adopted as infants often get little help in grappling with the special brand of grief sparked by the psychological loss of birth parents they never knew, the Boston psychiatrist says.

"Relatively few parents are equipped to help their kids face the depths of sadness that they often feel regarding this loss," Nickman holds.

Psychologist David M. Brodzinsky of Rutgers University in New Brunswick, N.J., estimates that about 25 percent of those adopted as infants develop serious psychological difficulties by adolescence, compared with 15 percent of nonadopted youngsters.

A number of factors play shifting roles in the emotional lives of adopted children, Brodzinsky holds. These include the social stigma attached to adoption (such as teasing by peers and awkward "family tree" assignments at school), feelings of loss about biological parents, traumatic separation from one or more caregivers for older adoptees, and genetic propensities for psychological and behavioral disorders inherited from biological parents.

Children who try to avoid thinking or talking about adoption issues, often in concert with their adoptive parents, most often fall prey to emotional problems and identity confusion, Brodzinsky suggests. He expands on this argument in Being Adopted:

The Lifelong Search for Self (1992, Doubleday), written with psychiatrist Marshall D. Schechter of the University of Pennsylvania School of Medicine in Philadelphia and science writer Robin Marantz Henig.

Shortcomings in the Search Institute survey render it difficult to interpret, according to Brodzinsky.

"This new study is important because it gets people talking about adoption," he says. "There's still little nonclinical research on adoption."

But more is on the way. A study submitted for publication by Sharma, Benson, and McGue compares 4,682 teenage adoptees recruited from public schools in 35 states with 4,682 non-adopted students matched for sex, age, and race. Overall, adoptees report small, but statistically significant, elevations in legal and illegal drug use, sadness and worry, and aggressive behavior, as well as slightly lower optimism about the future, academic achievement, and parental support and closeness.

Teens adopted as infants display overall psychological adjustment comparable to that of nonadopted controls, Sharma says. Personal and family difficulties increase progressively for those adopted at later ages.

The findings underscore the need to move children quickly out of foster care into adoptive homes, according to the researchers.

Scientists also hope to move quickly toward a better understanding of adoptive families. "These studies are a few chips off a massive block from which we're trying to remove a true representation of adoption," Sharma contends.

4

"Many adoptions fail when children are unable to bond with their new parents."

ADOPTION IS NOT APPROPRIATE FOR SOME NEEDY CHILDREN

Jodie Gould

Adoption is often advocated as a means of helping the thousands of children who languish in the foster care system. In the following viewpoint, however, Jodie Gould describes several families who faced extreme difficulties and even physical harm due to their emotionally disturbed adopted children. Some abused and neglected children have been so traumatized that they are unable to live normal family lives, Gould explains. She concludes that people considering adoption should find out as much as possible about a child before adopting. Gould is a freelance writer in New York City who specializes in women's and family issues.

As you read, consider the following questions:

1. What is an "unattached" child, and what usually happens to such children, according to Gould?
2. Why is it difficult to obtain information about an adopted child's past, according to the author?
3. On what basis does Larry Gellerstein oppose the right of adoptive parents to refuse adopted children, as quoted by Gould?

From Jodie Gould, "When Love Is Not Enough: The Tragedy of Adoptions That Fail," *Family Circle*, July 19, 1994. Reprinted with permission of *Family Circle*; ©1994 by Gruner + Jahr USA Publishing.

The kitchen of Margaret Jochims' home in Broken Arrow, Oklahoma, was warm with the smell of baking bread. It was the Sunday before Christmas in 1986, and Margaret had just returned from taking David, her 6-year-old adopted son, shopping for winter clothes. Although they'd been married for 15 years, Margaret, then 33, and Bob Jochims (pronounced YOKE-um), 34, hadn't wanted to start a family. But through a friend who worked in the state's department of human services, they'd heard about older kids needing homes and decided they wanted to help.

It was David's third week with the Jochims. As Margaret removed the loaf from the oven, she thought about how well the adorable sandy-haired little boy seemed to be adjusting to his new home. He was chatty and friendly, and best of all, he'd begun calling them "Mom" and "Dad" soon after they picked him up from the adoption agency.

Her thoughts were interrupted by a crashing noise coming from the attached garage. She ran in and saw her husband's workbench in flames. She remembered that Bob, who had gone skiing for the week, had changed the oil in the car before he left, and she feared the remaining unopened cans of oil might catch fire and cause the garage to explode.

With no time to panic, Margaret quickly backed the car out of the garage. Then she ran back in, grabbed the fire extinguisher and tugged unsuccessfully at the release pin. Her face burned from the heat as the flames climbed menacingly toward the roof of the house. Tossing the extinguisher aside, she turned on the garden hose and drenched the blaze with a steady stream of water. Minutes later, fire trucks blasted into the driveway.

A FIRESTARTER

She was thankful that David was off riding his bike in the neighborhood, and she watched alone as the firefighters hacked away at what remained of the garage. Had she waited a minute longer, the house would have been destroyed too. The fire had been deliberately set, the marshal told her afterward. In disbelief, Margaret noticed David's new mittens—the ones he'd said he hated but she'd bought anyway—charred and lying near a box of matches on the workbench. She knew immediately who was responsible.

When the boy returned, Margaret confronted him. "David, do you know how this fire got started?" she demanded.

"No," he said and shrugged. "It must have been something in the garage." Then Margaret told him she saw that he had set fire to his mittens. "It's no big deal," David said. "It's just a fire."

He never admitted to causing the fire that resulted in $6,000 in damage and nearly cost the Jochims their home. "I was stunned by his indifference," Margaret says. "I just couldn't deal with him and the fire at the same time. I let it slide because I thought it was probably an accident. You know, kids do play with matches." Heeding the advice of the fire marshal, they registered David in a five-week course in fire safety at the local fire station.

After the holidays the Jochims enrolled him in first grade. Since Margaret worked full time as a medical secretary and Bob was a computer analyst, the boy stayed for the after-school program. At school David's behavior, once called "mischievous," got worse.

"He lied constantly to his teachers," Margaret says. "And he wouldn't sit down in class. I started getting phone calls saying he was stealing things from the other children. He even tried to stab another kid with scissors. It was upsetting to me, but we felt he was a normal kid who was just having trouble adjusting."

A Disparity of Expectations

In truth, adoption—whatever the age or circumstances of the child—is not a simple solution to any problem: it always carries its own complications. . . . When adoptive families come to grief, it is often from a disparity in expectations: either the parents expected something the child can't deliver, or the child delivers something the parents didn't expect. Much of the blame for this should be shifted to agencies, who ought to know better. . . .

Particularly when agencies may be reluctant to predict (and, to be fair, they are never entirely able to) how a given child will adjust to his adoptive family, prospective parents need to think carefully about what they can put up with.

Katharine Davis Fishman, *Atlantic Monthly*, September 1992.

But David was apparently anything but normal. Soon Margaret was being called to school nearly every week. He would get F's in conduct while earning A's in reading and math. Exactly one month after the fire, he was suspended for flooding the boys' bathroom. When asked why he did it, he simply replied, "Because I wanted to."

In February the Jochims took David to a private therapist, who described him as deeply troubled. "We began to understand that this was a pattern, and that he wasn't able to function in a normal setting," Margaret says. "That's when I became truly frightened."

Several months later, with no improvement in his behavior, the school suggested David meet with its own psychologist. Surprisingly, the psychologist made his diagnosis after just one session. David, he believed, was a paranoid schizophrenic who should be placed in an institution, not with a family.

When the Jochims told their private therapist what the school's psychologist had said, the therapist agreed with the diagnosis, but said he wouldn't recommend moving the boy to an institution. "Can you give us any hope that he will make it through life at all?" Bob pleaded. "Can we get him through school, at least?"

The therapist chose his words carefully: "I envision that David may not make it through school, and that he might be in prison before he turns 18."

Bob and Margaret returned home to digest the news. "We were just blown away," Margaret recalls. "We knew David had problems, but it was difficult to accept that a psychologist thought he should be institutionalized, and that no amount of love would change that."

A History of Abuse

David's problems were not surprising given his horrendous past, only a portion of which the Jochims knew when they adopted him. According to Donna Rust, the social worker who had arranged the boy's placement with them, David and his two siblings were taken from their mother when David was 3 because of sexual and physical abuse. He was then placed in a series of foster homes, where he also may have been sexually molested.

Although the Jochims had submitted to a "home study" (a requirement in most states for adoption), during which their own backgrounds and fitness as parents were ascertained, they had not asked for details of David's background, and social workers had not volunteered much information. (An Oklahoma law now requires all known information about a child's health and family history to be disclosed before an adoption is made final.) But in their excitement to adopt, the Jochims naively thought, "How many problems could a little boy have?"

Adoptions through licensed agencies require a waiting period before they become final. During this period, which lasts 6 to 18 months depending on the state, a social worker visits the family several times to determine if the placement is working. (Laws governing independent adoptions, which are arranged through an attorney, vary from state to state.)

For Bob and Margaret, this requirement now meant the difference between a several-month trial period and a lifelong commitment. "I haven't bonded with David," Bob admitted. "I can give him up."

But Margaret could not. "I don't want to be another person to turn my back on him," she sobbed.

By the spring of 1987, Margaret found it increasingly difficult to function at work. David burned a mark on their car's steering wheel and sneaked into a neighbor's house to play with her toddler's toys. Still, it was not enough to make Margaret change her mind.

The Turning Point

"Then one day I noticed a neighbor's car door was open," she recalls. "I went over to shut the door, and I saw the car's cigarette lighter lying in the driveway. I looked in the car and there were burn marks all over the dash and seat. I was so distraught I walked around the block and found another car's door open. David had done the same thing."

This was the turning point for her. "We had him for five months," Margaret says. "Bob and I realized we had no control over him and things could only get worse. It was so hard to give him up. We prayed about it and thought about it and finally made a decision."

Margaret called Donna Rust. The Jochims knew that David had been adopted before and returned, but now Rust told Margaret some disturbing details as to why. With several previous placements, he had been sent back after just one weekend: He'd acted out sexually as well as showed inappropriate sexual behavior toward his sister. (As far as the Jochims know, they were the first couple with whom David had been placed by himself.)

The agency personnel had withheld this information, Rust admitted, because they wanted the boy to have a fresh start. "The state is now very open about that sort of thing," says Rust, who no longer works for the department of human services. "They make every effort to give adoptive parents the information they need."

Bob describes David's last day with them as being "like a funeral." Two days earlier, they'd sat him down at the kitchen table to review the events of the previous five months. They told him that they loved him, but that he needed more help than they could give. David was silent. Afterward, he got up from the table and went to his room.

"If he was upset, he didn't show it," Bob recalls. "If he'd cried and said he didn't want to go, it would have torn us up more. I don't know if we could have gone through with it."

While the social workers put his toys and suitcases in their car, the Jochims said their final goodbyes. "We hugged him and told him again that we loved him," Margaret says. "David didn't even turn around to wave when they drove away. After he left, I was hysterical; Bob was crying too. He thought it wasn't going to be hard for him, but it was. Bob and I just held each other for a long time."

UNATTACHED CHILDREN

Of the 100,000 adoptions that take place in the United States each year, approximately 25 percent are of "special needs" children—the majority of whom are classified as such merely because they are over the age of 3. According to Richard Barth, professor of social welfare at the University of California, Berkeley, the older the child is at the time of placement, the more likely the adoption will fail. Children 3 through 5 have a less than 5 percent failure rate; the rate for children 13 or older is 24 percent.

Many adoptions fail when children are unable to bond with their new parents, often because of prior sexual and physical abuse. Most of these "unattached" children end up in institutions or group homes or are funneled back into the overburdened foster-care system.

Ken Magid, chief of psychological services at Golden Medical Clinic in Golden, Colorado, explains why bonding with a parent is so critical to a child's development. "The bonding process is the fundamental building block for all future relationships and the establishment of trust, love, competence and healthy self-esteem," says Magid. "Many children who have pathological problems have probably had breaks in this attachment cycle. Left untreated, many unattached children will grow into psychopathic adults."

How can prospective parents guard against adopting a high-risk child and suffering the heartbreak the Jochims experienced? Laws regarding disclosure vary from state to state, and the type of information adoptive parents can receive about a child's background is not always available, especially if the adoption is independent. Since independent adoptions are under less scrutiny by state licensing agencies, parents must rely on whatever information their lawyer provides.

MICHAEL

This was the situation for Joelene and Rick Beeman of Mt. Vernon, Washington. The Beemans, who have four biological daughters, hired a lawyer and adopted a 3-year-old boy named Michael in March 1986. "We couldn't get any information on Michael because his mother gave birth to him at home with an unlicensed midwife," explains Joelene, 37. "Then she abandoned him at a day-care center when he was 2."

Almost immediately, the chubby, blue-eyed little boy began lying, stealing and voraciously eating, even food still in its wrapping or obviously spoiled. He would fly into violent rages, his small body infused with the strength of someone twice his age. Yet it took the Beemans several more years to discover the extent of Michael's problems.

"When he was 5, he took one of those toy Fisher-Price people, put a string around its neck and hung it in a window," Joelene recalls. "I got really upset and asked him, 'Do you know what happens when you hang somebody?' He said, 'Yeah, it kills them.' I asked him why he wanted to kill this guy, and he said, 'Because he was naughty.'"

By age 6, Michael had threatened suicide; and by the time he was 7, he had killed the family cats and a pet chicken. "The first cat he killed was our oldest daughter's kitten," Joelene says. "He was mad at my daughter, so he went out and took a baseball bat to the cat. The next cat he killed was pregnant. He admitted that he kept kicking it. We were all devastated."

Eventually, Michael's targets moved from animals to his sisters. "We have a travel trailer, and the girls were sleeping in it while we were remodeling their bedroom," Joelene recalls. "One night they smelled gas. We found out Michael had turned on the propane tank. If they had fallen asleep, they wouldn't have awakened the next morning. Later he asked me, 'Why are you mad at me?' I said, 'What do you mean? You tried to kill the girls!'"

SEVERELY UNATTACHED

In 1992, the Beemans placed Michael in the Intermountain Children's Home in Helena, Montana, where he remained for two years. They spoke to him once a week by phone and visited him every three months. The doctors there diagnosed him as "severely unattached" due to a prior history of sexual and physical abuse and neglect. They also believe he may have fetal alcohol effect, a difficult-to-diagnose birth defect caused by a mother's heavy drinking during pregnancy.

Unfortunately, the Intermountain program did nothing to reduce his aggressive and violent behavior. Michael, now 12, is currently in a private treatment center in Seattle, where he continues to act out, both violently and sexually. In the last six months, he has even had to be confined to a "safe room" several times. Michael has not been home for a visit with the Beemans since May 1993. During that weekend, another of the family's cats disappeared.

"I'm afraid of the future," Joelene admits. "Our insurance only covered part of his treatment, so we had to give up partial custody of Michael in order for the state to help us. We no longer have a say about what happens to him. They were thinking about placing him in a foster home, but I'm afraid he'll hurt someone as soon as he gets out. The Intermountain Home wouldn't recommend that he be committed because he hasn't been given a chance to assimilate into society. The only other option is to bring him back home, which isn't possible, given his mental state. My daughters are terrified of him, and frankly, so am I."

THE OPTION TO SAY NO

Larry Gellerstein, a supervisor at the Downey Side Families for Youth adoption agency in New York City, says there are no warranties on adoptions. Gellerstein, who has been an advocate for older-child adoptions for 21 years, feels that some parents use the right of refusal in adoptions as an opportunity to keep searching for the "perfect" child.

In 1989 Gellerstein received a call from Nancy and William Brown (not their real names), two wealthy attorneys in their late 30's. The Browns had adopted a blue-eyed, honey-haired newborn boy through an independent adoption. Six months later, the child was diagnosed with cerebral palsy. Gellerstein referred the Browns to professional help.

"They called me a month later, saying they'd done everything I had suggested, and that adoption was just not for them," Gellerstein recalls. Concerned for the child's welfare, he started pursuing other families who might adopt the baby. "The other couples all said 'yes' until I mentioned the child had cerebral palsy, then they declined on the spot," he says. After months of rejection, Gellerstein and his wife, Eileen, decided to adopt the little boy themselves. They named him Scottie.

Then the Browns tried another private adoption and again encountered a medical problem. This infant had a minor neurological disorder that caused involuntary shaking in one leg. The spasms would not affect the child's ability to walk. Fearing the condition would get worse, the Browns asked if the birth mother would take the baby back. She did.

"I don't believe parents should have the option to give their adoptive children back," Gellerstein says bitterly. "When you adopt, you are saying that you have agreed to take this child into your home and care for this child regardless."

But Linda Zuflacht, executive director of Adoption Services Associates, a national adoption agency in San Antonio, Texas, disagrees. She believes it's important that prospective parents have this option. "Agreeing to raise someone else's biological child is an enormous hurdle for many couples," Zuflacht says. "If there's something about the child the parents just can't live with, the child won't grow up in a good home."

Margaret Jochims cautions adoptive parents to learn as much as possible about the child and birth parents before signing the papers. A year after David left, the Jochims adopted a 10-year-old girl, Julie, and, a year later, an 11-year-old boy, Michael. Both were from the same agency as David.

"We really wanted to help the kids," explains Bob Jochims of their decision to try again. "The social worker assured us that the second time would be different. We were afraid, but we were more aware of our next two kids' backgrounds, and we asked a lot more questions."

The Jochims last saw David a few months after they gave him back in 1987—on *Waiting Child*, an Oklahoma TV show featuring children who are available for adoption through the department of human services. Then 7, he eerily appeared on the screen wearing a plastic firefighter's helmet. The Jochims were told that shortly afterward, David was committed to the Children's Medical Center in Tulsa for a year. They believe he is currently in a foster home somewhere in Oklahoma.

"The idea that they could put him into the system and do this to him—and to us—is appalling," Margaret says. "I don't regret getting to know David, and I don't think Bob does either. But I can't say we weren't relieved when he was gone."

> "The best—indeed, the only—way
> to protect our children is to increase
> radically the resources available."

EFFORTS TO HELP ABUSED CHILDREN MUST BE INCREASED

Andrew Vachss

Andrew Vachss is an attorney in New York City whose only clients are children. He is the author of the novel *False Allegations* and of numerous articles on child abuse. In the following viewpoint, Vachss argues that in recent years the media have downplayed the problem of child sexual abuse by highlighting the stories of a few individuals who have been falsely accused of abusing children. He insists that children continue to be victimized and that more resources—such as money, time, and skilled workers—must be employed to ensure the safety of the nation's children.

As you read, consider the following questions:

1. How are child abuse cases different from other cases, in the opinion of the author?
2. According to Vachss, why can children no longer rely on parents' instincts for protection?
3. What specific proposals does the author make to help reduce child abuse?

From Andrew Vachss, "If We Really Want to Protect Children," *Parade*, November 3, 1996. Reprinted with permission from *Parade*, copyright ©1996.

S ome people will tell you that there was no such thing as child sexual abuse a few short decades ago—the "good old days." And if you go to the files and read the old newspapers, you might well believe them.

Unless you were a victim, now grown to adulthood.

Then the media "discovered" child abuse. Like a pendulum, press coverage swung from one extreme to the other. From being reported so rarely that many doubted its very existence, child abuse became such a frequent subject of coverage that rarely a day went by without new accounts of horrors.

Now the media spotlight has been turned on defendants who maintain that they have been falsely accused of sexually abusing children—and the media backlash is so strong that you might well believe that we are in the midst of a modern-day Salem witch hunt.

THE OSTRICH APPROACH

Here's the truth: The battle against child sexual abuse is no "witch hunt." In Salem, there *were* no witches. In 20th-century America, sexual predators *do* exist—in alarming numbers.

Blaming the media won't make the problem go away. The media didn't invent child sexual abuse, and it can't make it disappear. Nor will our collective wishing make it do so. In fact, taking the ostrich approach actually benefits predators. Ignorance helps them to multiply, and cowardice makes them strong.

There are far more people who love and respect children than there are those who prey upon them. But if that is so, why aren't we winning this battle? Because, with all the media muddle surrounding child abuse, we are losing confidence in our collective ability to find out the truth.

How do we learn that truth? How do we protect our children?

A child abuse case is never a level playing field. It is never a fair fight. Why? What is so special about children that we treat these cases differently from other vicious crimes? Is it true that children's "memories" are different from those of adults? That children are easily "brainwashed" or cannot distinguish between truth and fantasy? Or is it that children are perceived as property, as lesser citizens, because of their age? Do we fear the inadequacy of their memories—or the truth of them?

I have never yet met an abused child (of whatever age) who was not crying to be heard and to be believed, to be validated and (eventually) assured that there was nothing "special" about him or her that brought on the abuse—that the child was simply a "parent's" (or other predator's) target of opportunity.

Child abuse cases *are* different, in part because the stakes are so much higher. If an adult is the victim of a crime, even if the defendant is acquitted, the adult is as "free" as the perpetrator. But in a child abuse case, the consequences of an improper acquittal are often that the victim is returned to the abuser.

The major difference between child abuse cases and all others is this: Those who make the decisions—be they judges, juries, social workers, police officers or the general public—too often act as though the "issue" were on trial, not the facts. But child sexual abuse is not an "issue," like capital punishment or abortion or gun control. Child abuse is a fact—a hideous, foul fact that traumatizes our culture just as it traumatizes individual victims.

If we want the truth about child sexual abuse, there is just one thing we can do: Look only at the facts of each individual case. It is not a question of "believing" children, or of "believing" in "witch hunts" or "false allegations." It is, and always will be, a question of fact-finding.

ACTIONS, NOT INSTINCTS

It sounds cold-blooded to say this, but a wrongful conviction of child abuse can be reversed. The damage from a wrongful acquittal probably cannot. Unless and until we learn to judge, case-by-case—unless and until we work to create a climate in which the facts will be found—countless victims will continue to be doomed.

Protecting one's own children is a biological imperative—it is how our species sustains itself. When an animal fails to protect its babies, they do not survive. And so the negative characteristics of that unprotective parent are not carried forth into new generations.

But it doesn't work that way with human beings. Our minds have evolved ways to sustain ourselves even when we ignore our biological imperatives. Children can no longer rely on our "instincts" for protection. Only our *actions* can achieve that goal.

For every parent who violates the sacred trust *every* child represents, there are thousands committed not only to protecting their children but also to protecting *all* children. That desire is our highest calling. The actual expression of that desire defines the character of each individual. And we can only truly express such a desire with behavior—rhetoric won't get the job done.

Healthy, happy, productive children—children who evoke their maximum potential—are no accident. They are not some fortuitous result of randomly scattering seeds on unnourishing ground. No, such children are always a harvested blessing, deeply dependent on climate and care. We create that climate and that care; and its most precious, indispensable element is *safety*.

Calling children "our most precious resource" is easy. Treating them as such is the key to our species.

More cases of child sexual abuse are *never* reported than are *ever* tried. Yes, some people are wrongfully convicted. And we must do our best to see that this never happens and to rectify it when it does. But no child benefits from being forced to carry the banner of a false allegation. Being made to do so is, in itself, a pernicious form of child abuse. And, every day, innocent victims are being ignored even when their cases do come to court.

MORE RESOURCES NEEDED

What happens to those children?

Your children, America.

We need to pay what it costs to find the truth, because we can't afford what it costs not to. The best—indeed, the *only*—way to protect our children is to increase radically the resources available.

We need therapy for all children who are the subject of child abuse allegations, regardless of any jury voting "guilty" or "not guilty."

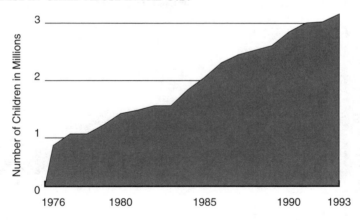

RISE IN CHILD ABUSE IN THE U.S.

Source: U.S. Department of Health and Human Services, National Center on Child Abuse and Neglect.

We need better investigations. That means better investigators. And that means comprehensive training. It means adequate pay, competent supervision and full accountability. It means the use of standardized protocols, so that the outcome depends on the facts, not on the individual perspective of the investigator.

We need an objective "one-stop shop" system to avoid the confusion that results from subjecting a child to a series of interviews. All cases would be referred to a multidisciplinary resource center which has no vested interest in the outcome and which has the sole job of finding the facts. No party to the case—be it prosecution, defense, a parent in a custody battle or otherwise—would be permitted to control the investigation. A full and complete record should be made available to all once it is finished.

For children especially, investigative interviewing to determine the likelihood of sexual abuse is an inherently intrusive and often traumatic experience. Because they want the pain to stop, many children go "mute" or "stop remembering," making it appear that they are changing their account of the events. And any such disparities can easily be exploited.

We need a system in which only wrongdoers fear the consequences.

It took an informed and enraged nation to pass child labor laws. It will take no less to protect children from an even more horrific societal crime.

We humans have been on the planet a long time. If we forget where we come from, if we forget our own children, then our evolution is not "in progress"—it is finished.

"Within this [child protective services] system, children have less protection than an accused murderer."

EFFORTS TO PREVENT ABUSE TOO OFTEN HARM CHILDREN

Hannah B. Lapp

In the following viewpoint, Hannah B. Lapp argues that government child protection agencies have become overzealous in their attempts to combat child abuse. She contends that such agencies often falsely accuse parents of abusing their children. In many cases, Lapp maintains, children have been removed from their homes for extended periods of time and subjected to unpleasant living conditions, unnecessary psychiatric medication, and undeserved punishments. Lapp, a dairy farmer and freelance writer in Cassadaga, New York, suggests that the needs of children would be better met if child welfare officials made more of an effort to keep troubled families together.

As you read, consider the following questions:

1. How does the author describe the altercation that occurred between Billy Stefan and his father on May 28, 1992?
2. According to the author, what is the rationale behind letting the court decide what action is in "the best interest of the child"?
3. How are children's rights violated by child protective services in Arizona, according to that state's Civil Liberties Union, as cited by Lapp?

Excerpted from Hannah B. Lapp, "Child Abuse: In the Name of Protecting Kids from Harm, Social Workers Subject Them to Cruel and Unusual Punishment," *Reason* magazine. Reprinted by permission of *Reason*.

The first time I heard of Billy Stefan's plight, he had just celebrated his 15th birthday at a Bradford, Pennsylvania, children's home. Family members had visited him, bringing lots of birthday presents. But for Billy, it all ended in tears. "Daddy, why can't I go along home?" he had pleaded.

It was Billy's determination and that of his older brothers— Tom, 17, Kevin, 19, and Ron, 20—that convinced me to include their case in my research on abuses by child-protection agencies. Their father, Donald, who owns a welding business in Yorkshire, a small town in Cattaraugus County, New York, had sought help from several of the numerous advocacy groups that fight arbitrary official intervention in families. My sister, Barbara Lyn Lapp, runs a chapter of one such group, Victims of Child Abuse Laws (VOCAL), in nearby Chautauqua County.

Donald Stefan's grievances were not much different from the hundreds of others heard each year by organizations like VOCAL: The state had cried child abuse; the parent had cried foul. Then I saw copies of letters the boys had written their family-court judge during the time they were separated from their father and institutionalized. The case cried out for answers. Why, in this era of emphasis on children's rights, did the desperate pleas of two teenaged boys go unheeded?

THE CHILD ABUSE INDUSTRY

The bureaucracy in which the Stefan family finds itself mired is a formidable system, supported by billions of dollars in federal and state funding each year. Federal law requires every state to have an agency within its Department of Social Services that fights child abuse. Usually called Child Protective Services, this agency has offices in every county. Among other things, CPS caseworkers are supposed to identify children who are suffering abuse, remove them from their homes if necessary, and seek a family-court order to place them in a safer environment.

Within this system, children have less protection than an accused murderer, a civil defendant, or even a target of asset forfeiture. A child can be removed from his home at a caseworker's discretion; the government need not show probable cause. To keep him locked away from his family indefinitely, the Department of Social Services attorney need only convince a judge by "a fair preponderance of the evidence"—a much weaker standard than "beyond a reasonable doubt"—that the child is neglected or in danger at home. Parents are generally represented by an attorney who rebuts the state's case. Although the judge appoints a "law guardian" to serve as the child's advocate, the child is usually not present, and his wishes count for little or nothing. All this is done under a legal cloak of secrecy, ostensibly to protect the child.

Author Mary Pride calls the CPS system "The Child Abuse Industry" in a 1986 book by that title. Others who have investigated its performance describe it as chaotic and inept. But the CPS system usually avoids scrutiny by hiding behind secrecy laws. To examine the flesh-and-blood consequences of child-protection policies, we have to ask those who have been inside the system: the social worker who gives up her job to break the silence, the parents who protest, and the children whose interests the system is supposed to promote. Their testimony contradicts the government's claim that it is helping families and protecting children from abuse.

A FATHER-SON SCUFFLE

Billy was 14 and his brother Tom was 16 on May 28, 1992, when two Cattaraugus County CPS employees, flanked by police, descended on their country home and took them away. Their case became one of the 136,000 reports recorded by the New York State Central Register for Child Abuse and Neglect that year. The person who placed the call to the CPS hotline remains anonymous.

Donald Stefan and his wife, Linda, had been having marital problems for several years; they were separated on and off. But Donald didn't expect Linda's sudden accusation that he had beaten and molested his son. Much less did he expect that CPS would accept such a claim without talking to the rest of the family.

The Stefans recall an altercation between Donald and his youngest son the day Billy was alleged to have been beaten, but no one other than Linda felt it constituted abuse. Billy and his father, interviewed separately, call it a "spanking" in response to foul language the child had used, and both admit it developed into a father-son scuffle. According to Billy and numerous people who saw him on the day of the incident and the day afterward at school, the confrontation left him with one visible mark, a small scratch on his cheek.

But Linda, who was not a witness, gave a very different account of the incident, portraying it as a serious assault. And Billy, who says his mother paid him to lie, initially confirmed that his father had sexually abused him. (He later recanted and, together with his brothers, rose to his father's defense.) The authorities moved immediately to pick Billy up.

PROFOUND STUPIDITY

Billy was placed in a "safe house" with his mother, and his older brother Tom volunteered to go along because he felt Billy needed him. "We were both crying," Tom remembers. "Billy didn't want to go, but Chuck Talbot [their caseworker] said they'd put him in a foster home if he didn't get in the car." Standing by in disbelief were the boys' older brothers and cousins, an aunt, and their grandmother, Effie Stefan, all of whom were more than willing to take care of them. In the weeks that followed, the Cattaraugus County Department of Social Services, which oversees CPS, would cut Tom and Billy off from contact with all relatives except their mother; shuttle them from one institution to another, including a mental hospital; "treat" them with psychotropic drugs; send the police after them when they tried to escape; and subject them to physical abuse—all without hearing the boys or their family (other than Donald and Linda) in court.

A VIOLATION OF PARENTAL RIGHTS

Nationwide, between 60 and 65 percent of all child abuse reports are closed after an initial investigation determines that they are "unfounded" or "unsubstantiated.". . .

The determination that a report is unfounded can only be made after an unavoidably traumatic investigation that is inherently a breach of parental and family privacy. To determine whether a particular child is in danger, caseworkers must inquire into the most intimate personal and family matters. Often it is necessary to question friends, relatives, and neighbors, as well as school teachers, day-care personnel, doctors, clergy, and others who know the family.

Laws against child abuse are an implicit recognition that family privacy must give way to the need to protect helpless children. But in seeking to protect children, it is all too easy to ignore the legitimate rights of parents. Each year, about 700,000 families are put through investigations of unfounded reports. This is a massive and unjustified violation of parental rights.

Douglas J. Besharov with Lisa Laumann, *Society*, May/June 1996.

Advocates of the family-court system believe the task of determining "the best interests of the child" should be left to caseworkers, court-appointed psychologists, court-appointed law guardians, and the court itself. When the Stefan boys and others like them appeal to public officials, they are told, in essence, that children don't know what's good for them and can't handle open court, so they'd better leave such matters to those who know better. Chautauqua County Social Services Commissioner Edwin Minor dismisses complaints about arbitrary removals of children from their homes with this assertion: "All children want to return home; the more abused they are, the stronger is their desire to go back."

Added to the profound stupidity of children as envisioned by Minor et al. is the mindset propagated by our modern child-saving movement, which suspects every parent of child abuse and portrays the family as "the most dangerous institution that exists" (the view of a psychologist who appeared on a PBS documentary). The thrust is clear: We can't trust anyone—except the government and those it empowers to determine "the best interests of the child." Furthermore, the issue of child abuse is supposed to be so sensitive that it can be dealt with only in secret by family court and social-service departments. Unfortunately, these agencies have often demonstrated that they can be trusted more to enhance their own images and paychecks than to serve the needs of children. . . .

A SYSTEM THAT DOESN'T WORK

The General Accounting Office reports that the number of children in foster care rose 55 percent between 1985 and 1991. The number will continue to rise, the GAO says, as long as the federal government pays for removing children from their homes but not for services that might keep a troubled family together.

Vincent Fontana—who boasts that his 30 years of work against child abuse have brought children to the point where they can say to their elders, "Don't hit me, or I'll call Dr. Fontana"—is himself troubled at the system he helped to create. He admits that we have all the same problems we did decades ago, before an intense child-abuse awareness campaign, and he's frustrated: "It's a system that doesn't work." Some experts are calling for a total rebuilding of the nation's child-protection system. Says the National Center for Child Abuse and Neglect: "The CPS system is like a 911 number that cannot distinguish a murder in progress from littering."

In Arizona, the state Civil Liberties Union issued a report in 1992 condemning the violation of children's rights by CPS. Among the problems cited are the incommunicado isolation of children, CPS workers who are cynical and offer no hope to families, and court records contaminated by a host of facts that do not prove child abuse (such as the bathing of a 4-year-old child by his parents, or kissing and hugging "too much" during visits). "Once the child is removed," the report states, "the system will go to any lengths to sustain their charges, even in the face of copious evidence they have made a mistake." The report also cited experimentation on children with treatments given sex offenders, including the use of penile devices, nude photographs, and noxious odors.

DRUGS AND PUNISHMENT

In 1992 New York state's Commission on Quality Control released a report that criticizes the liberal use of psychotropic drugs on children in state mental-health facilities. In 51 percent of the cases examined by the commission, children were drugged without the consent of a parent or guardian. Only 33 percent of children receiving anti-psychotic medications had a diagnosed psychotic disorder. Both Tom and Billy Stefan were treated for acting up with potent psychoactive substances that have numerous possible side effects, including fainting, heart failure, confusion, agitation, seizures, and psychomotor and mental retardation. Both boys experienced some of these symptoms after being drugged. Neither of them had needed psychiatric medication before they were removed from their home.

The Commission on Quality Control also criticized the frequent use of punishments that deprive children of essential family and social contact. Although the commission found that children in state institutions were well cared for physically, the report concludes that "in a real sense these children are often deprived of their childhood, first by the desperate conditions in their family lives, and then by the very design of the service systems."

New York Commissioner of Social Services Mary Jo Bane complained that "the report's caustic criticism and the condemnation of the whole system is not justified." She objected to the suggestion of local oversight panels, saying that "decisions regarding child placement should be left to the party with the legal authority to act." Bane's defensiveness reflects the main problem in the child-welfare system: power without accountability. Officials are always promising reform, but nothing ever changes that fundamental reality.

One former CPS worker describes the system as "a world all its own . . . like being in the high school gang: either you play their game, or you're out." The weak ethics and ignorance of family realities among members of her CPS unit didn't matter, she says. What mattered was maintaining the gang and the "'let's go get 'em' mentality." This social worker put conscience over career and dropped out.

In fairness, her description of apathy and incompetence does not apply to all caseworkers; the problem with the CPS system is not personnel. The problem lies in assuming that we can safely hand over broad powers to government without public over-sight and constitutional constraints. The kind of reforms being proposed by social-service agencies do not address this issue at all. Rather, they involve expanded government powers and in-creased funding. Without radical reform, kids like Billy Stefan will continue to wait for relief.

> "Ratification of the convention by the
> United States would have a dramatic
> effect on how the world looks at the
> way children are treated."

U.S. RATIFICATION OF THE U.N.
CONVENTION ON THE RIGHTS OF THE
CHILD WOULD BENEFIT CHILDREN

Robert F. Drinan

The United Nations Convention on the Rights of the Child was
adopted by the U.N. General Assembly in 1989 and has been ratified by most of the world's 193 nations. The convention requires governments to commit to providing children with their
basic nutritional, educational, and health needs. As of 1997, the
United States had not ratified the agreement. In the following
viewpoint, Robert F. Drinan argues that by ratifying the convention, the United States would send a strong message to the
world that the needs of children are an important priority. Drinan is a professor of law at the Georgetown University Law Center in Washington, D.C.

As you read, consider the following questions:

1. What statistics does the author cite concerning the condition
   of children around the world?
2. What does Article Four of the convention require, according
   to Drinan?
3. What steps have been taken to improve the lives of children
   in various parts of the world, as described by the author?

From Robert F. Drinan, "Proclaiming the Rights of Children," *America*, August 31, 1996.
Reprinted by permission of the author and *America* magazine.

The U.N. General Assembly adopted the Convention on the Rights of the Child in 1989; as of March 1, 1996, 187 of the world's 193 nations had ratified it. That makes this convention the most rapidly accepted human rights treaty in history.

The Holy See was one of the convention's principal advocates. The Vatican representative at the United Nations, Archbishop Renato Martino, signed the convention in April 1990, and the Holy See became the fourth nation in the world to ratify it. Later, Archbishop Martino stated that "by choosing to be among the first in acceding to the Convention on the Rights of a Child, the Holy See encourages all countries and peoples to join in assuring legal protection and effective support to the well-being of all of the children of the world."

In November 1993 Pope John Paul II, speaking in Rome to an international conference, expressed the hope that the Convention on the Rights of the Child "may soon become the first universal treaty on children's rights." He continued with a plea: "To this end, I reiterate the urgent invitation to the leading nations to hasten ratification of this Convention. . . ."

NUTRITION, EDUCATION AND HEALTH

The United States signed the convention in 1995, but has not yet ratified it. This is attributable to the fact that some conservative American groups have wrongly contended that the treaty could be "anti-family." What does the treaty involve? By agreeing to the 30 articles in the convention, nations commit themselves to furnish the basic elements of nutrition, education and health to all children.

Since the convention came into force, there have been great improvements in the condition of children around the globe. But the fact remains that nearly 200 million of them in the developing world are malnourished, 30 percent do not complete even four years of schooling and an estimated 20 percent do not have access to basic medical care. Worst of all, 40,000 children die needlessly each day.

Recognizing the still deplorable state of the world's children, Article Four of the convention requires nations to undertake appropriate measures, to the maximum extent of their available resources and, where needed, within the framework of international cooperation. Experts on the convention agree that this language, as well as the letter and spirit of the treaty, imposes an obligation on the poor nations to place a first call on resources for their children. It also implies a duty on the part of rich nations to assist the less developed countries to carry out their new pledge to children.

The principal instrument for monitoring the implementation of the convention's articles is the U.N. Committee on the Rights of the Child. Two years after ratification and regularly thereafter, each country is required to submit a detailed report concerning its compliance. Some 43 countries have now complied with this requirement. Their reports have been carefully reviewed and aggressively challenged by 10 experts who constitute the membership of the committee.

Although it is too early to judge how much the committee has been able to accomplish, it is clear that the landscape on how the world judges children and their rights is changing. Fourteen of the 43 nations reporting have incorporated provisions of the convention into their own constitutions. Of the 43 nations that have reported, moreover, 35 have passed new laws or amended existing ones to conform with the convention.

Everywhere in the world there are new initiatives and energy devoted to improving the status of children. The movement is strengthened by more than 50 non-governmental groups dedicated to advancing children's rights. In 1996 UNICEF [United Nations International Children's Emergency Fund] issued a 54-page brochure entitled The Progress of Nations that documents some of these developments. The list is impressive. Several countries have recently taken constructive steps to phase out child labor. In compliance with the convention, Indonesia has increased the length of compulsory education from six to nine years. Several nations have overhauled their systems of juvenile justice. A third of the 43 countries examined to date have built the Convention on the Rights of the Child into their educational curriculum.

One of the benefits of the work of the Committee on the Rights of the Child is the extensive documentation that is now available. It is possible, for example, to compile charts showing the level of a nation's compliance with the global standards. Non-governmental groups are more and more using this information to mobilize the shame of the world against nations that do not respect the rights of their children.

MISTREATMENT OF CHILDREN IN THE UNITED STATES

Although the United States is not yet required to report to the committee, the world cannot be unaware of the ways in which the richest nation mistreats its children. From 1969 to 1986 the percentage of children living in poverty in the United States increased from 13.1 percent to 22.9 percent—by far the highest among all industrialized nations. Indeed, only four industrialized nations have child poverty rates of more than 10 percent. We must also bear the shame of being the nation whose affluent children are the most affluent in the world, while its poor children are the poorest, and the gap between them is the widest.

The United States was one of the leaders in developing the Convention on the Rights of the Child, but we have not contributed to the funding by rich nations that is essential if the covenant is to be effective. In 1969 the U.N. General Assembly endorsed a target of 0.7 percent of the G.N.P. as the minimum for aid by developed nations. In 1994, the United States ranked last among 31 donor nations.

Not a "Children's Liberation Charter"

The Convention is in no way a "children's liberation charter", and neither does its existence or content deny or reduce the importance of the family. This is clear when the Convention is—as it must be—read as a whole. However, there have been attempts in certain quarters to prove the contrary by pinpointing selected provisions which, taken on their own, could be interpreted as being hostile to parents and the family or designed to bestow on children a questionable level of autonomy. It is important to remember that the spirit and letter of the Convention are in no way intended to do either.

Nigel Cantwell, Defence for Children International Webpage, 1997.

The world press has not yet made use of the vast data bank on the plight of children being compiled by the committee. But human rights academics and activists are writing about the tragedies that are being revealed concerning street children, children exploited by employers, children required to participate in war and children handicapped for life by land mines, flawed nutrition and inadequate schooling. Perhaps some day a child like Anne Frank will write a book about the scars and sorrows of the neglected children of this world.

The fact that virtually all nations have committed themselves to comply with the newly mandated standards related to the rights of children may not produce an immediate elevation in the conditions affecting them. But solemn promises made by nations do have a way of raising their standards of behavior. This is particularly true when there is a U.N. committee to monitor compliance.

Ratification of the convention by the United States would have a dramatic effect on how the world looks at the way children are treated. The vast array of agencies devoted to children in the United States could use the U.N. committee as both a new listening post and a pulpit to preach about America's neglect of its own youngest citizens.

It is encouraging that the nations of the earth have for the first time in history solemnly pledged to guarantee the observance of a comprehensive code on the rights of children. Humanity has thereby committed itself to bringing about an era when humanity's most precious and vulnerable human beings are offered the protection they need and deserve.

| "The U.N. Treaty on the Rights of the
Child is a bad deal for Americans on
every count."

U.S. RATIFICATION OF THE U.N. CONVENTION ON THE RIGHTS OF THE CHILD WOULD THREATEN AMERICAN FREEDOMS

Phyllis Schlafly

Phyllis Schlafly is the author of numerous books on national defense, foreign policy, and social issues. She is a lawyer, syndicated columnist, radio commentator, and president of the Eagle Forum, which publishes the monthly *Phyllis Schlafly Report*. In the following viewpoint, Schlafly criticizes the United Nations Convention on the Rights of the Child, an international treaty that requires signatory governments to ensure that children receive health care and education. She contends that if the United States ratifies the convention, the U.N. will gain control over the education and health care of America's children. Granting such power to the U.N., Schlafly maintains, would undermine the rights of American parents to raise their children in accordance with their personal beliefs and values.

As you read, consider the following questions:

1. For what two reasons is it important to carefully scrutinize international treaties, in the author's opinion?
2. What concerns does Schlafly have regarding the treaty's articles on the content of education?
3. On what grounds does the author oppose the creation of a committee to enforce the U.N. convention?

From Phyllis Schlafly, "The New World Order Wants Your Children," *Phyllis Schlafly Report*, March 1993. Reprinted with permission.

The Children's Defense Fund (CDF), the chief vehicle for those who want government to take over the raising of children, has a new goal under the Clinton Administration. Having failed to get Congress to pass the costly ABC Child Care bill, the CDF is now pushing to get a United Nations treaty on children signed and adopted so that child-advocacy lawyers can assert "children's rights" against their parents. Since Hillary Clinton was chair of CDF's board of directors from 1986 to 1991, and since she was succeeded as CDF chair in 1991 by Donna Shalala (now secretary of The U.S. Department of Health and Human Services), and since CDF's CEO, Marian Wright Edelman, is Hillary's close friend, we can anticipate an aggressive effort by the Clinton Administration on behalf of this treaty.

The treaty is called the United Nations Convention on the Rights of the Child. It was unanimously adopted by the U.N. General Assembly on November 20, 1989, and signed by more than 100 foreign governments. President George Bush did not sign the Treaty or send it to the Senate for ratification. There are dozens of excellent reasons to reject it.

If the text of the U.N. Treaty were proposed as new federal legislation, the bill would never pass. It would be unacceptable to the American people because it would give the Federal Government too broad a grant of power over our children, families and schools, and it would be unconstitutional because of both vagueness and federal interference with states' rights.

But the treaty has been blessed by the United Nations and layered with lofty goals and high-sounding words. Its salesmen are peddling it with pathetic stories of the mistreatment of children, such as outrageous murders in Bolivia. CDF and 150 liberal advocacy groups in the United States have made it a "cause" and are even using it as a litmus test to try to label Congressmen as "pro-children" or "anti-children."

TREATIES SHOULD BE CAREFULLY ANALYZED

It is always important to scrutinize proposed treaties even more carefully than ordinary legislation, first, because treaties can be ratified at any time by two-thirds of U.S. Senators present and voting (e.g., with two Senators voting aye and one Senator voting no), and second, because of the preferential status which treaties enjoy in the American system of government. Once ratified, they become part of the "supreme law of the land," along with the U.S. Constitution and federal laws.

Any time a treaty is proposed, we should study the language, as well as the intent, and consider a worst case scenario of how the treaty's provisions—in the hands of international bodies (over which we have no control)—could imperil American sovereignty and the rights of American citizens.

The American philosophy of government, as spelled out in the Declaration of Independence and the United States Constitution, is that the individual's inalienable rights to life, liberty and property come to each of us from our Creator and may not be impaired without due process of law, and that the prime purpose of government is to guarantee those rights. Americans do not believe that individual rights originate with the government, the United Nations, kings, rulers, or even society.

The United States Constitution lists several rights that Americans can assert *against* our government; then the Ninth Amendment adds, "The enumeration in the Constitution of certain rights shall not be construed to deny or disparage others retained by the people." The U.N. Convention on the Rights of the Child, on the other hand, purports to be a comprehensive listing of *all* rights of the child, and is based on the concept that a child's rights originate with the U.N. Treaty itself or with the government. The logical conclusion is that a child would have no rights except those in the Treaty, and what government gives, government also can take away.

If this U.N. Treaty is ever written into American law—a treaty which assumes that government is the source of the listed "rights"—this can only diminish the status of existing American rights. Since U.N. treaties, courts, and bureaucracies do not respect our American philosophy of individual rights, it would badly curtail our liberty to submit ourselves to a U.N. document interpreted by foreign lawyers.

WHO WILL ENFORCE THE RIGHTS?

The next problem with the U.N. Convention on the Rights of the Child is, who is to be the enforcer of the Treaty's rights— and against whom are they to be enforced? In American constitutional law, the right of free speech, for example, is a right which the individual can assert against government encroachment. This U.N. Treaty doesn't say who is to enforce the child's rights against whom, but it is reasonable to infer that many of these rights are to be enforced against the parents, probably with the help of government.

The Treaty purports to give the child the right to express his own views freely in all matters (Article 12), to receive information of all kinds through "media of the child's choice" (Article 13), to freedom of religion (Article 14), to be protected from interference with his correspondence (Article 16), to have access to information from national and international sources in the media (Article 17), to use his "own language" (Article 30), and to have the right to "rest and leisure" (Article 31).

What do all these rights mean, how will they be enforced, and against whom? Does this mean that the child can refuse to do his homework and household chores because they interfere with his "right" to rest and leisure? And can he demand a government-paid lawyer to file a lawsuit against his parents?

Reprinted by permission of Chuck Asay and Creators Syndicate.

Does this mean that a child has the right to use his native language in school and cannot be required to speak English? Does it mean that a child can demand the right to watch television in order to receive media reports from national and international sources?

Does this mean that a child can assert his right to say anything he wants to his parents at the dinner table? Does this mean that the government will assist the child to join a cult or select a different church from the one his parents attend? The U.N. Treaty does not provide answers to these questions.

These are just a few of the literally dozens of brand new "rights of the child" scattered throughout the 54 Articles of the U.N. Treaty, which is longer than the entire U.S. Constitution.

Despite a vague reference to undefined "rights and duties of parents," the Treaty does not recognize any specific parental right to make decisions for their minor children.

THE GRAB FOR POWER OVER EDUCATION

Suppose Congress were to consider legislation to set up a procedure for the Federal Government (or the U.S. Department of Education) to define the content of the education of every child. Imagine the howls that would go up as parents and concerned citizens protest that Congress has no business prescribing school curriculum. From all sides, we would hear citizens reassert their dedication to local control of education. Private schools would express fear that they would become an endangered species.

The U.N. Convention on the Rights of the Child prescribes the content of what must be taught to all children in several sensitive areas. Article 28 prescribes that "the education of the child shall be directed to" such things as "the principles enshrined in the Charter of the United Nations"; respect for "the national values of the country . . . from which he or she may originate, and for civilizations different from his or her own" (that means adopting the controversial curricular approach known as "global education" or "multiculturalism"); "equality of sexes" (that means promoting the Equal Rights Amendment which was rejected by the American people in 1982); and "the development of respect for the natural environment" (certainly one of the most politically-charged issues in the United States).

The U.N. Treaty recognizes that private schools may exist, but only so long as they teach the above subjects and otherwise conform to government standards.

The American people would not permit Congress to prescribe what all our children must learn on these sensitive issues, so we certainly don't want the United Nations to lay down the law. But, if this U.N. Treaty is ratified, dictatorial control over all school curriculum will become part of the supreme law of the land.

In several sections, the U.N. Treaty imposes on the government the obligation to "strive to ensure," to "render appropriate assistance," and to "take all appropriate measures" so that children may enjoy certain economic benefits. Article 4 states that the government "shall undertake all appropriate legislative, administrative, and other measures" to implement "economic, social and cultural rights." Furthermore, the government "shall undertake such measures to the maximum extent of their available resources."

These expensive responsibilities include "health care services" (Article 24), social security (Article 26), and an "adequate" standard of living, nutrition, clothing and housing (Article 27).

What does this language really mean? The big-spending liberals will surely argue that the Treaty will require our government to impose new taxes—or go further into debt—to carry out these obligations.

The U.N. Treaty would probably require us to set up a national system of daycare. Article 18 says that the government "shall ensure the development of institutions, facilities and services for the care of children . . . of working parents." The Treaty gives the children the right to benefit from these services and facilities.

What does the U.N. Treaty mean when it requires universal legal standards for the care and protection of children against neglect, exploitation, and abuse? Is it "neglect" not to establish government daycare centers? Or is it "neglect" to put children in daycare centers where they are exposed to more illnesses? Shall we leave this up to United Nations judges or "experts" to decide?

The Treaty even obligates the government to ensure "standards" for child care institutions, services and facilities. National daycare standards were part of the ABC Child Care bill and were a major reason why, after lengthy debate, Congress specifically rejected this approach in its 1990 legislation. Are we now to have Congress overridden by a United Nations mandate?

The U.N. Treaty grants the child the right to be protected against neglect or negligent treatment (Article 19). Could homeschoolers be charged with "neglect" for not sending their children to an institutional school? Or for not sending children to school until age seven or eight?

OPENING UP NEW LITIGATION

Unlike our U.S. Constitution, which only mentions rights that can be enforced against the government, the U.N. Treaty declares "rights of the child" against parents, the family, private institutions, and society as a whole. Since the Treaty is a legal document which, if ratified, would become part of the "supreme law of the land," we can expect ACLU [American Civil Liberties Union] lawyers to bring a series of test cases to see how far the courts will extend its provisions. The Convention would open up a Pandora's box of litigation, either in some international court or in U.S. courts, or both. It's hard to say which venue would be worse.

International courts are frequently biased against Americans. Several years ago when the World Court treated the United States unfairly, the Reagan Administration simply thumbed its nose at the Court. Another administration might have acquiesced in the unfair treatment. Every day, U.S. courts hand down decisions which become law in our country, and it is not in the interests of American citizens to have those decisions grounded in United Nations treaties rather than in U.S. constitutional law.

Americans will be in for a shock if judges around the country start applying this U.N. Treaty as the supreme law of our land. It is full of vague requirements which are susceptible to different and even contradictory interpretations.

For example, Article 24(3) requires the government to "take all effective and appropriate measures with a view to abolishing traditional practices prejudicial to the health of children." What kind of standard is that? The practice doesn't have to be harmful or even negligent, but merely "prejudicial," and this new "standard" would be defined by unelected judges.

What will it mean to enforce Article 28, which makes "primary education compulsory and available free to all"? Will that make it compulsory to give subsidies to private or religious schools—and if so, will they be required to modify their religious practices? Or, will Article 28 ban private and religious schools altogether? Either outcome would override existing Supreme Court decisions. Do we want United Nations courts to answer these questions?

Of course, all these grandiose U.N. Treaty goals would not be complete without the establishment of a new international bureaucracy and mechanism of control. The U.N. Convention on the Rights of the Child would set up a Committee on the Rights of the Child consisting of ten "experts" chosen by secret ballot from a list of nominees submitted by the governments that sign the Treaty. Of course, there is no assurance that any American will be on this committee of experts, not even any assurance that even one "expert" will be friendly to American institutions and traditions. (Articles 43 and 44)

The Secretary-General of the United Nations will provide "the necessary staff and facilities" which will assist the committee of experts in monitoring and reporting on "the degree of fulfillment of the obligations" established under the Treaty. We cannot assume that this would be merely an expensive exercise in international busybodyism, because this is not merely a treaty of generalized hopes; it is full of mandatory words such as "rights" and "obligations.". . .

The U.N. Treaty on the Rights of the Child is a bad deal for Americans on every count. It should never be signed by our President or ratified by our Senate.

PERIODICAL BIBLIOGRAPHY

The following articles have been selected to supplement the diverse views presented in this chapter. Addresses are provided for periodicals not indexed in the *Readers' Guide to Periodical Literature*, the *Alternative Press Index*, the *Social Sciences Index*, or the *Index to Legal Periodicals and Books*.

Janice Arenofsky	"Adoption: Teens Talk About Their Experiences," *Current Health 2*, March 1996.
David Blankenhorn	"Pay, Papa, Pay: Where Have All the Fathers Gone?" *National Review*, April 3, 1995.
Hillary Rodham Clinton	"The Fight over Orphanages," *Newsweek*, January 16, 1995.
Charles Doersch	"Bring Back the Orphanage?" *Scholastic Update*, March 10, 1995.
Jane Haddam	"Promote the General Welfare," *Nation*, January 29, 1996.
Albert R. Hunt	"A Much Needed Rally for Children," *Wall Street Journal*, May 30, 1996.
Val J. Peter	"Welfare Reform, the American Family, and Orphanages: What's Best for the Children?" *USA Today*, November 1995.
Katha Pollitt	"Adoption Fantasy," *Nation*, July 8, 1996.
Ann Slayton	"First Things First: Paternity and Child Support for Nonmarital Children," *Children Today*, January/February 1993.
Sheryl Stolberg	"Foster Care Rules Left Out Family, Tragedy Followed," *Los Angeles Times*, November 30, 1991. Available from Times Mirror Square, Los Angeles, CA 90053.
Barbara Nevins Taylor	"'I Can Make It on My Own,'" *New York Times*, September 16, 1994.
Dave Thomas	"Every Child Deserves a Family," *Family Circle*, November 21, 1995. Available from 110 Fifth Ave., New York, NY 10011.
Tommy G. Thompson	"Response and Responsibility: Welfare Reform That Works," *Common Sense*, Spring 1994.
Cheryl Wetzstein	"Verdict on Teens Adopted at Birth: The Kids Are All Right," *Insight*, August 8, 1994. Available from 3600 New York Ave. NE, Washington, DC 20002.

CHAPTER 4

WHAT CAN SOCIETY DO TO IMPROVE THE WELFARE OF CHILDREN?

CHAPTER PREFACE

At the 1996 Democratic national convention, Hillary Rodham Clinton spoke about the rights and needs of children. She quoted the African proverb "It takes a village to raise a child" to emphasize her belief that America's children need the help of parents, teachers, government, and all of society to thrive. A few weeks later, at the Republican convention, presidential candidate and former senator Bob Dole responded, "It doesn't take a village to raise a child. It takes a family."

Many liberals agree with Clinton, arguing that society and the government have the responsibility to help needy parents care for their children through programs that supply them with food, money, job training, and other forms of aid. In addition, these commentators assert, society must provide all children with an education and must step in to protect children when they are being abused by their parents or other adults. According to this view, children belong to all of society, and it is the responsibility of everyone in the "village" to ensure that children are properly cared for.

On the other hand, many conservatives insist that the responsibility for the upbringing of children belongs to parents alone and that parents have the right to raise their children in the manner they believe is appropriate. These commentators contend that government institutions, in their efforts to help children, often violate parents' rights and intrude on the sanctity of the family. For example, these critics accuse the public education system of teaching children values that their parents find offensive. They also insist that child protection service agencies frequently remove children from their homes based on unfounded reports of abuse. Outraged by what they see as excessive government intrusion in family life, conservatives such as Dole argue that government should step aside and allow parents to raise their children as they see fit.

The authors in the following chapter present a wide range of ideas on how to improve the welfare of children. Some advocate new programs, such as job training for youth, while others focus on inspiring parents and other individuals to take more responsibility for society's young people.

"If this nation can't stand for its children, it doesn't stand for anything."

AMERICANS SHOULD WORK TOGETHER TO IMPROVE THE LIVES OF CHILDREN

Marian Wright Edelman

Marian Wright Edelman is the founder and president of the Children's Defense Fund, a Washington, D.C., child advocacy group, and the author of *Families in Peril: An Agenda for Social Change*. In the following viewpoint, which is excerpted from a speech she delivered at the National Summit on Ethics and Meaning in Washington, D.C., in April 1996, Edelman maintains that the United States does not adequately care for its children, especially those who are disadvantaged. She concludes that Americans should call for a renewed commitment to ensure that the needs of all children are met.

As you read, consider the following questions:

1. What statistics does the author cite as evidence that the welfare of American children is threatened?
2. What religious analogies does Edelman use to further her point?
3. According to the author, what are some of the specific issues that the nation should address?

From Marian Wright Edelman, "Putting Children First," *Washington Monthly*, July/August 1996. Reprinted with permission from the *Washington Monthly*. Copyright by The Washington Monthly Company, 1611 Connecticut Ave. NW, Washington, DC 20009, (202) 462-0128.

R ecently, a young mother walked into a WIC office—
Women's, Infants', and Children's Nutritional Program office—seeking help to feed her hungry baby. When an overworked and tired WIC worker saw the baby drinking from a
bottle of red liquid, she was about to read the mother the riot
act. Just as she was about to scold her, the mother broke down
in tears. She had run out of money a week ago, hadn't eaten in
three days, and had used her last money to buy baby formula,
which had run out the day before. She knew her baby needed to
eat, so she had gone to McDonald's and filled the baby's bottles
with two free things: Ketchup and water.

Do you think, as our political leaders on both sides of the
aisle seem to be thinking these days, in the congressional proposals we've been debating, and as most of our governors and
mayors and county executives too frequently do—do you think
that this hungry baby is responsible for America's ills? For our
budget deficit, crime problems, and poor education systems?
For the structural changes, wage stagnation, and our labor mar-
ket, the de-industrialization of our cities, and the economic
blight in many of our rural areas? Do this baby and desperate
mother have any control over the downsizing of giant corporations, the replacement of human workers by technology, or the
exportation of jobs abroad and our global economy?

Is this baby—who had a one-in-three chance of being born
without timely prenatal care in the world's leader in health technology, and a one-in-four chance of being born poor in the richest nation in history—the cause or the victim of the widening
income gap between rich and poor, which allows 23,000 poor
families with children to live on less income in 1993 than one
entertainment industry executive? Did this baby manufacture or
sell the more than 222 million guns circulating in our nation today, that kill an American child like her every hour and a half?

I find it unbelievable that the morally unthinkable killing of
children has not only become routine, but is increasing in our
democracy. We're number one in the world as a military power.
Are we saying that we are helpless to keep our children safe
from the gun violence that kills them every hour and a half in
our nation? Gun deaths among our children almost doubled
over the last decade; among Blacks and Black teenagers, the increase was 294 percent. I think we can do better.

BABIES ARE SACRED GIFTS
Did this baby contribute to the pervasive breakdown of moral,
family, and communal values in our too selfish and secular cul-

ture? And is this baby responsible for her mother's and father's behavior or poverty, or ours?

This baby didn't vote for Democrats, Republicans, independents, liberals, or conservatives, cannot make campaign contributions, lobby, or hold press conferences to make her needs known. . . .

This baby, like my child and yours, and the grandchildren I hope to have and that some of you are lucky enough already to have, is a sacred gift of a loving God, and a citizen of the wealthiest nation in the world. Denying her food, preventive health care, the chance to get ready for and learn in school, access to safe child care if her parents work outside the home, education to prepare her for the next century, and jobs after that education, and safety from violence is immoral and lacks both common sense and budget sense.

© Boileau/Rothco. Reprinted by permission.

Blaming and punishing this baby—as our political leaders, in our names, have been trying to do—for our personal or collective discontents, for our shortcomings and the unfairness of our economy, for short-term political or economic gain contravenes the Old and New Testaments, the American covenant that we honor so well in words but so poorly in deeds.

We're a nation that professes to honor our Judeo-Christian tradition. If I can be forgiven by the rabbis for paraphrasing the midrash, it has been said that when God was bargaining with the people of Israel about whether He was going to give them the Torah, He demanded adequate guarantors. The people of Israel initially offered God their elders, but God held them to be insufficient guarantors. They then offered God their prophets, but God said no, that that wouldn't do either. And it was only when their children were offered as guarantors, with the promise that they would be taught God's word, that He agreed to share the Torah.

And when Jesus Christ invited little children to come unto him he did not invite only rich or middle-class, white, male children without disabilities from two-parent families, or our own children, to come. He welcomed all children, and so must we.

And so I hope that we will come together across race and class and religion and faith and age, and stand up for all of our children, in word and deed. We want parents and grandparents and religious and community leaders to come together. Because as tough as times are, and as hard as so many parents are struggling to make ends meet, I think we can all do better. And it's time to hold ourselves to a higher standard, in our homes, communities, private sector, and government at all levels. That's what we're coming together to say.

We may not be able to agree on a lot of things as Americans, but I hope that . . . we will say that as Americans we are going to agree that as a nation and as a people, we're not going to do harm to children. And that we're going to invest in what our children need, to get a healthy and a fair and a safe start.

Standing for Children

So we are asking all young and middle-income working families who are struggling to make ends meet, despite declining wages and economic insecurity—if you're worried about these things for yourself and your children, please come and stand with us. If you are as troubled as I am by the pollution of our airwaves, air, water, food, and earth, and our children's values, come and stand with us. If you're worrying about whether your children's schools are preparing them for the twenty-first century, whether there's going to be a job afterward, come stand with us. If you're anxious about your children getting sick—I, as a mother, find it unthinkable that if my child got sick I couldn't take him to the doctor, a problem so many millions of families face. It's obscene that our political leaders are not debating how we get health care to every one of the 10 million children who don't have it, but how to take away health care from millions more. If you think that's wrong, then come and stand with us.

And if you are tired of our political leaders talking about family values and about children, while cutting things families need to raise healthy and educated children, then come and stand with us.

If this nation can't stand for its children, it doesn't stand for anything.

Let me end with a prayer, as I always do, to ask God to forgive our rich nation, where small babies die of cold, quite legally. May God forgive our rich nation, where small children suffer from hunger, quite legally. God forgive our rich nation which lets our children be the poorest group of citizens, quite legally. God forgive our rich nation that lets the rich continue to get more at the expense of the poor, quite legally. May God forgive our rich nation, which thinks that security rests in missiles rather than in mothers, and in bombs rather than in babies. May God forgive our rich nation for not giving you sufficient thanks by giving to others their daily bread. God help us never to confuse what is quite legal with what is just and right in your sight. Everything that Hitler did in Nazi Germany was legal, but it was not right.

Let's come together in a massive moral witness to make sure that our nation does what is just and right for our children.

| "Licensing would hold a parent responsible for competency rather than leaving children to endure incompetent parenting."

LICENSING PARENTS WOULD HELP CHILDREN

Jack C. Westman

Many policy makers advocate a parental-rights amendment to the Constitution as a means of protecting the right of parents to raise their children free from government intrusion. In the following viewpoint, Jack C. Westman opposes such a measure and argues instead for a policy designed to secure the right of children to be raised in safe and healthy environments. Specifically, he calls for requiring parents to obtain parenting licenses. In order to get a license, Westman maintains, individuals should be required to receive parenting education and to pledge to adequately nurture their children. According to Westman, licensing parents would ensure that children are given the care they need to develop into healthy and productive adults. Westman is a professor of psychiatry at the University of Wisconsin, Madison, and the author of *Licensing Parents: Can We Prevent Child Abuse and Neglect?*

As you read, consider the following questions:

1. What should government do to support competent parents, in the author's view?
2. How would the enactment of parental-rights legislation affect society's ability to protect children from abuse, in Westman's opinion?
3. What "paradigm shift" is required for society to accept licensing parents, according to the author?

From Jack C. Westman, "No: License Parents to Insure Children's Welfare," *Symposium*, *Insight*, May 15, 1995. Reprinted with permission from *Insight* magazine. Copyright ©1995 by News World Communications, Inc.

O f the People, the parental-rights organization, correctly faults local school policies that exaggerate the rights of children and minimize the rights of parents on such issues as sex education, condom distribution and health care. But the parental-rights movement mistakenly assumes that the schools or the government are trying to take over parental responsibilities. Of the People implies that child rearing is strictly a family responsibility.

As the National Commission on Children reported to then-President George Bush and Congress in 1991, "It is a tragic irony that the most prosperous nation on Earth is failing so many of its children. Solutions will depend upon strong leadership and the concerted efforts of every sector of society—individuals, employers, schools, civic, community and religious organizations, and government at every level."

TOO MANY PARENTS ARE INCOMPETENT

In recent years schools and protective services for children have become involved in family affairs because too many parents are unable—or unwilling—to direct the upbringing and education of their children. For example, the Center for Children of Incarcerated Parents reports that 1.5 million children have an imprisoned parent. The Carnegie Corp. of New York concludes that "millions of infants and toddlers are so deprived of loving supervision, intellectual stimulation and medical care that their growth into healthy and responsible adults is threatened."

A growing number of incompetent parents are unable to handle responsibilities for their own lives, much less for their children's lives. They neglect and abuse their children physically, emotionally and sexually, as defined by state child neglect and abuse statutes. According to data collected from the 50 states by the National Center on Child Abuse Prevention and Research, annually substantiated cases of child maltreatment rose from 690,840 in 1985 to 1,016,000 in 1993, an increase of 47 percent. My analysis of this data reveals that some 2.7 million incompetent parents have both neglected and abused 3.6 million children.

Some social theorists have blamed this behavior on the stresses of poverty, racial discrimination and unemployment. But most parents who live in poverty, experience racial discrimination and are unemployed do not neglect and abuse their children. The direct cause of child neglect and abuse is incompetent parenting.

Incompetent parents contribute to the deterioration in the quality of public education and public safety throughout our nation, forcing the government to intervene in family life. Because that intervention often is ineffective, one in three neglected and abused children grow up to be violent, habitual criminals and welfare-dependent members of our society.

Our society clearly has a stake in competent parents who care about what happens to their children and who can restrain themselves from harming them. The financial benefit of competent parenting can be estimated by calculating the average contribution of productive citizens to our economy and the cost of incompetent parenting tallied by calculating the average loss of productive income and direct expenditures on habitual criminals. I estimate that competent parents contribute $1 million to our economy for each child they rear. Incompetent parents cost society $2 million for each child they neglect and abuse. The best social program for any child is a competent parent.

RECONCILING PARENTS' AND CHILDREN'S RIGHTS

Parental rights and children's rights can be reconciled. The parental-rights amendment reinforces the expectation that the responsibility falls on parents to protect their children from our hostile and exploitative society. But nonparenting adults and community organizations also have a responsibility to model positive social values for children. The National Task Force for Children's Constitutional Rights, based in Litchfield, Conn., seeks an amendment to the Constitution that assures that every child shall "enjoy the right to a safe and healthy home, the right to adequate health care, the right to an education, and the right to the care of a loving family." If enacted, the amendment would reduce the pressure on all of us to create a benevolent society that protects and nurtures our young. [The amendment was not enacted.]

The rhetoric of the parental-rights movement suggests that government is the enemy of parents. Far from it: Government can and should do more to support competent parents by controlling inflation, giving families income-tax credits and the aggressive pursuit of child support. Competent parenting is a legal right in the sense that incompetent parenting, as shown by child neglect and abuse, is a cause for state intervention and the possible termination of parental rights. Child-labor laws, mandatory education laws and child abuse and neglect laws reflect the principle that children have rights and are not owned as property by their parents.

Government can prevent incompetent parenting by pursuing antiaddiction measures that reduce demand for illegal drugs and by aggressive law enforcement to make neighborhoods secure. In the educational realm, courses that discourage teenage pregnancy, reinforce abstinence and teach contraception will make better parents and stronger families.

Our government also should protect the civil rights of children to competent parenting, according to numerous bills of children's rights and a series of White House conferences on children. As efforts to overcome racism and sexism have shown, the implementation of any civil right requires regulation; not everyone is influenced by persuasion and education. A clear statement of each child's right to competent parenting with enforcement capacities is needed to signify that competent parenting is valued by our society.

THE FREEDOM TO ABUSE CHILDREN

Still, as it is now in the United States, any male or female at any age can assert comprehensive parental rights over a child they conceive, without the expectation that they should be competent to parent that child. They are free to neglect and abuse the child until the child demonstrates sufficient evidence of damage to warrant state intervention. Then the state attempts to prove that the parents are unfit—and also may be obliged to defend parents who are eligible for public defenders.

A parental-rights amendment does nothing to ensure that all children are competently parented. If enacted, it would make it more difficult to enact laws that protect children before neglect and abuse occur, and it would impede efforts to make parents more accountable for the care of their children. For example, in 1989 California enacted a law requiring parents of children with behavior problems to attend parent-teacher conferences at public schools. This is an instance of the helpful hand of government that the amendment would tie.

LEGAL STANDARDS FOR PARENTING

The amendment also would preclude setting standards for parenting. A proactive approach to the problem of dysfunctional families is for states to set legal standards for parenting. This would place the primary responsibility for child rearing with parents rather than with the state by default. Just as individual responsibility for driving a car is certified by a driver's license, the individual responsibility of a parent for child rearing would be certified by a parenting license. Then all parents, at least in principle, would be capable of directing the upbringing and education of their children.

Public and private agencies carefully screen adoptive and foster parents. State governments license every activity that affects other persons, and children are persons. Yet licensing parents unnecessarily evokes fears of governmental control of child rearing and of undue restriction of individual freedom. It requires a paradigm shift to seeing parenting through the eyes of children, not just the parents.

With a licensing process the question of parental competence would be faced before, rather than after, a child is damaged by neglect or abuse. Licensing would hold a parent responsible for competency rather than leaving children to endure incompetent parenting until they publicly exhibit signs of injury or neglect.

THE RIGHTS OF BABIES

Providing healthy and successful rearing environments for the millions of American children now being incompetently reared will be very expensive, but not providing them will be more expensive still. . . .

The only long-term solution, I believe, is Jack C. Westman's proposal that we require prospective parents to meet the same minimum requirements that we now expect of couples hoping to adopt a baby: a mature man and woman, sufficiently committed to parenthood to be married to each other, who are self-supporting and neither criminal nor actively psychotic. Such a licensure requirement would offend those who believe that people have an inalienable right to produce as many babies as they wish, no matter how incompetent, immature, abusive, or depraved they may be. . . . I am more concerned about the rights of those helpless babies than I am about the alleged procreative rights of their feckless parents—and about the lives of crime, violence, and social dependency that most of these babies are doomed to lead when they grow up.

David T. Lykken, Society, November/December 1996.

The initial requirement for a parental license would be the capacity to assume full responsibility for one's own life. Eighteen would be a reasonable age based on physical, social and emotional maturation and the likelihood of completion of high school. Parental or parental-surrogate assumption of responsibility for a minor and a minor's child would be required.

The next requirement would be the parent's pledge to care for and nurture the child and to refrain from abusing and neglecting the child. If this pledge was broken at a later time, the intervention upon a parent's rights would be based upon the failure of that parent to fulfill a contractual commitment to the child. The license would be revoked, rather than subjecting the parent and child to a quasi-criminal proceeding for termination of parental rights, as now is the case.

The third requirement would be completion of a parenting course or its equivalent. Family-life education already is provided in many communities and schools. Every high school in the country would require courses that prepare young people for the responsibilities of parenthood.

When vulnerable parents are identified by failing to meet these criteria, they would receive help. If they are unable or unwilling to adequately parent their children, existing child abuse and neglect laws would be enforced with timely termination of parental rights and adoption of the children.

However, the licensing of parents would entail little more administrative structure than currently is involved in marriage licensing, birth registration and existing protective services for children.

SHARING THE VISION

Licensing parents has little chance of gaining popular support—unless all of the organizations who speak for children and parents envision what life would be like in the United States if every child had competent parenting. If they all share that vision as an ultimate goal, they will find common ground.

Of the People and the National Task Force for Children's Constitutional Rights should unite in formulating a constitutional amendment that affirms that all children have the right to competent parents who direct their upbringing and education. Such a commitment would profoundly benefit all of our lives and future generations.

| "Very early intervention . . ., in the form of parental education, is a sound investment."

PARENT EDUCATION HELPS CHILDREN

Joy M. Rouse

In the following viewpoint, Joy M. Rouse describes Parents as Teachers (PAT), a Missouri-based program that provides education in child development and parenting skills to parents of children aged five or younger. Rouse contends that the PAT model, which has been adopted in forty-four states and four foreign countries, has been proven to reduce child abuse and improve the intellectual and social abilities of children. Rouse is a contributor to *Spectrum: The Journal of State Government*.

As you read, consider the following questions:

1. What are the four components of the PAT program, according to Rouse?
2. What have some of the studies of PAT's effectiveness found, according to the author?
3. In what positive ways are parents affected by PAT, in the author's opinion?

From Joy M. Rouse, "Parents as Teachers: Investing in Good Beginnings for Children," *Spectrum*, Fall 1994. (Notes in the original have been omitted.) Copyright 1994, The Council of State Governments. Reprinted with permission from *Spectrum*.

A Missouri program to educate parents on child development has proven its worth in helping produce healthy, happy, well-educated children prepared to succeed in the world. The program's success has led to it being duplicated worldwide.

"By strengthening families' ability to nurture their children physically, emotionally and intellectually, the Parents as Teachers program increases the likelihood that children will grow up healthy and safe and successful."—Marian Wright Edelman, president Children's Defense Fund.

A CHILD'S FIRST TEACHER

Parents as Teachers (PAT) is built on the philosophy that parents are their child's first and most influential teachers.

That philosophy was expressed by Ernest Boyer, president of the Carnegie Foundation for the Advancement of Teaching: "The influence of parents is of utmost importance because the foundation for excellence in education must be laid in the home." Parents as Teachers is a partnership among the home, the school and the community designed to provide support for all parents as they give their child the best possible start in life.

"Beginning at the beginning" is the hallmark of Parents as Teachers, a completely voluntary program designed for all families with children from birth to age 5—from the time they enter the world until the time they enter school. From single adolescent parents to two-parent, well-educated families, PAT helps parents acquire the skills to help make the most of the crucial early learning years. The program covers child development and parent-child activities that encourage language and intellectual growth, curiosity and social skills.

By promoting parent involvement in learning from the onset, PAT puts children and their parents on the right track for later achievement in school. Parents as Teachers is the first step in ensuring that children will indeed enter the classroom ready to learn. All families with very young children are eligible for Parents as Teachers, regardless of level of income, education or age. PAT was not designed as a targeted program, although it has been successfully implemented with Head Start and Even Start children. The experience of providing PAT to a broad range of families has shown that need for support and assistance in the parenting role crosses all socioeconomic and educational levels. High-needs families are attracted into a nontargeted program because it does not imply inadequacy or "bad parenting." Their special needs are met through intensified service.

A Success from the Start

Begun in 1981 as a pilot project in four school districts in Missouri, PAT has grown to 1,450 programs in 44 states, Washington, D.C., and four foreign countries (New Zealand, Australia, England, St. Lucia). In 1972, the Missouri State Board of Education adopted a position paper on early childhood education, defining the role and responsibility of the public education system during the years when home is the child's school. This position was based on the belief in the critical nature of the first three years of life in terms of the development of major abilities. This is also the time when parents are forming and cementing their approaches to childrearing. After the successful completion of the PAT pilot in 1984, the Missouri General Assembly passed the Early Childhood Development Act, making Missouri the first state in the nation to mandate that every school district provide parent education and family support services, beginning at the child's birth, to interested parents. Funding was appropriated to serve 10 percent of the age-eligible population, meaning that in one year, PAT spread from four pilot projects to 543 PAT programs—a massive undertaking for PAT trainers.

Worldwide interest in Parents as Teachers resulting from independent evaluations of its effectiveness led to the establishment of the Parents as Teachers National Center in 1987. In an effort to create a structure that promotes the growth of PAT and helps it sustain its high quality through outreach, training, research and development, the National Center was incorporated as a nonprofit organization in 1990. A Board of Directors was established, comprised of influential national leaders actively involved in education, health, mental health, social services, business and government.

The PAT Model

Parents as Teachers is a national model, but at the same time is a local program. The basic PAT model is maintained by local PAT programs, but within that model adaptations can be made to meet the needs of individual communities. The Parents as Teachers model includes four components:

• Personal visits are held regularly with families and certified parenting educators trained in child development and home visiting. By far the most popular aspect of PAT, the personal visit allows the professional to individualize and personalize the Parents as Teachers program for each parent and child. Parents learn what they can expect from their child at each stage of development, and participate in appropriate parent-child learning activities.

• Group meetings for parents serve two major purposes: first, to create opportunities for families to share successes and common concerns about their children's behavior and development; second, to provide a vehicle for additional input from the staff and outside speakers. Parent-child activities are provided during many group meetings to reinforce the importance of family interaction.

• Developmental screening helps parents understand their child's specific strengths and delays in any area of development. Hearing, vision and immunizations are checked. The advantage of this approach is that the earlier any problems are detected, the more successfully they can be managed—and in many cases overcome.

• A referral network helps parents link with other resources within the community that provide services beyond the scope of Parents as Teachers. These may include speech and hearing clinics, diagnostic services, programs for children with special needs, lending libraries, health and mental health agencies, and social service agencies.

PROVEN EFFECTIVE

Experience has shown that Parents as Teachers can produce confident, competent parents and well-rounded, academically able children. A Native American mother said, "This program has changed my life. Now I believe I can be a good parent." Recent research backs up parents' belief in the program's effectiveness and long-term benefits.

In 1985, an independent evaluation of the New Parents as Teachers pilot project involved 380 first-time parents representing Missouri's urban, rural and suburban communities. This study showed that participating children consistently scored significantly higher on all measures of intelligence, achievement, language ability and positive social development in contrast with the comparison group and national norms. Parents were more knowledgeable about child-rearing practices and child development than were comparison parents, and were more likely to regard their school district as responsive to their children's needs.

A follow-up investigation completed in 1989 indicated that at the end of first grade, PAT children scored significantly higher than the comparison group on standardized measures of reading achievement and math achievement. Significantly higher proportions of parents of PAT children initiated requests for parent-teacher conferences, and were more likely to be involved in school activities.

After statewide expansion of the Parents as Teachers model, the Missouri Department of Elementary and Secondary Education initiated another independent evaluation: the second-wave study to examine the program's effectiveness with a broader range of families. Results of the 1991 evaluation of the PAT program's impact on 400 randomly selected families enrolled in 37 diverse school districts indicated that both children and parents benefited. PAT children performed significantly higher than national norms on measures of intellectual and language abilities, despite the fact that the sample was over-represented on all traditional characteristics of risk. More than half of children with observed developmental delays overcame them by age 3. There were only two documented cases of child abuse among the 400 families during the three years of the program. Parent knowledge of child development and parenting practices significantly increased for all types of families. . . .

LEARNING TO PARENT

Child rearing is not an innate skill, and several states are trying to help educate parents about parenting. Home visits by social workers or nurses are among the most promising methods. . . .

In Vermont someone from the state's Success by Six program first visits a home within two weeks of a baby's birth. "That gets us in the door at age zero instead of age five, so we can assess what families need," Governor Howard Dean points out. Visits may continue for up to three years. "It is so inexpensive," says Dean, "to take care of children relative to the other things we do, such as build jails and put up expensive social-service networks for runaway youth."

James Collins, *Time*, February 3, 1997.

Positive results continue to be reported by school districts in Missouri. A study of 22 small rural school districts in southwest Missouri showed that children who participated in PAT scored significantly higher on their kindergarten readiness tests in number concept, auditory, language and visual skills than a comparison group whose parents did not participate in PAT. Of the 516 participants, 224 qualified for free or reduced-cost meals at school. The Parkway School District in St. Louis County found that third-graders whose families had participated in PAT and screening scored significantly higher than nonparticipants on the Stanford Achievement Test, including significant differences on all subtests. The study also reported that PAT graduates were less likely to receive remedial reading assistance or to be held back a grade in school.

NEW YORK AND CALIFORNIA STUDIES

A study of children at risk for educational failure conducted by S. Drazen and M. Haust in the Binghampton City Schools in New York showed that mean scores were higher on kindergarten readiness tests for PAT participants, even though the comparison group had been in other early childhood programs. Welfare dependence within the PAT group dropped by 10 percent, while dependence nearly doubled for the control group by the child's first birthday. In addition, PAT children required approximately one-third less money to be spent on special education for them. The report concludes that "very early intervention which continues for more than one year, in the form of parental education, is a sound investment that earns back more than the money spent by the time the children are in first grade, three years after the program ended."

A California study of predominantly Hispanic families determined that PAT parents consistently scored significantly higher than a control group on measures of parenting behavior and knowledge of child development regardless of mother's ethnic background and age. Strong and consistent benefits were found for PAT children on all measures of child development.

FEDERAL FUNDING FOR OFF-SHOOTS

The highly acclaimed Parents as Teachers program has been recognized by the U.S. Congress as an effective program for families and young children. Three major pieces of federal legislation have included references to PAT, indicating the credibility of this program among U.S. policy-makers.

• The Goals 2000: Educate America Act authorizes funding for Goal 1: School readiness. Parents as Teachers is a research-based, cost-effective program for states to use to meet this first education goal. In addition, individual programs can apply for Goals 2000 funding under Title IV: Parental Assistance. Congress has appropriated $10 million for Title IV for fiscal 1995, which is to be used to improve parenting skills in meeting the education needs of children aged birth through 5. This includes establishing, expanding or operating Parents as Teachers programs.

• Parents as Teachers is eligible for funding under the Family Preservation and Support Services program in the Omnibus Budget Reconciliation Act of 1993. This program authorizes federal resources for states to promote community-based services to promote the well-being of children and families, using a collaborative approach. Congress has allocated $900 million over five years for this program.

• Parents as Teachers is eligible for funding under the Even Start program, authorized under the Elementary and Secondary Education Act. In addition, parental involvement in Chapter 1 schools can include opportunities for parents to learn about child development and childrearing practices beginning at the birth of the child.

MAKING GOOD PARENTS

Parents as Teachers is designed to empower parents to give their children a solid foundation for school and life success. It is built on the belief that all parents want to be good parents, and that all families have strengths. It is a program that helps parents recognize and appreciate their child's growing capabilities, and helps them capture the window of opportunity when their young child is ready to learn something new. Parents from around the world praise the Parents as Teachers program because it affirms their strengths, increases their confidence and competence, and helps them give their child the best possible start in life.

"If we are to see our children grow
into responsive members of society,
. . . we need to develop the strength
of principle to guide by example."

ADULTS MUST BE ROLE MODELS FOR CHILDREN

Montel Williams

Montel Williams is the host of a syndicated television talk show. In the following viewpoint, Williams argues that in order to help children grow into mature, healthy individuals, adults must model responsible behavior for them to emulate. He writes that when adults engage in irresponsible behaviors such as promiscuous sexual activity and drug use, children are likely to follow their example. Therefore, he contends, adults should work hard, support their families, and make positive contributions to society.

As you read, consider the following questions:
1. What adult behaviors are responsible for the increasing teenage pregnancy rate, in Williams's opinion?
2. Why are sports heroes not the best role models for children, according to the author?
3. What does the author mean when he discusses the "triumph in being an 'average' member of society"?

From Montel Williams, "Time for Adults to Look in the Mirror," *Los Angeles Times*, June 21, 1993. Reprinted by permission of the author.

E ver since I left the U.S. Navy to travel the country as a motivational speaker and now, as a television talk show host, I have become convinced that the children of this nation represent the answers to our troubled times of drugs and family despair and violence. Before any solution can be found, we as adults and parents must face the sobering fact that we are letting our children down.

We ask young people to do the right thing, to act properly, but we don't do the right thing and we don't act properly. If we are to see our children grow into responsive members of society, "Do as I say, not as I do" simply will not do. We need to develop the strength of principle to guide by example.

No Surprises

Take a hard look in the mirror, because our kids are nothing but reflections of who we are. Children take their cues from us. Teen pregnancy has risen in direct correlation to the escalating divorce rate in America; 60% of marriages end in divorce, and too many youngsters see their parents with multiple sex partners. We can't be surprised when teens are promiscuous or teen pregnancies skyrocket.

We place substantial blame on young people for our nation's consuming drug crisis, but it isn't kids who are flying in narcotics or laundering money. Drugs are an adult-originated problem, with tragic effects on our youth. Too often, television programs teach our kids that violence is the way adults settle a problem. Truth is, we should be relieved that kids do only a fraction of what we do a whole lot of.

Solutions Exist

The good news is that the solutions do exist to right our children's way. After providing education—an inalienable right of every child on Earth—it is our duty to demonstrate who the real role models are in society. Too many youngsters today mistake American sports heroes and entertainers for role models. Role models are individuals children can emulate, to whose achievements they can realistically aspire. Role models are hard-working men and women who can explain how they got from A to Z in their lives. Heroes are great; we need heroes, but they can't always explain their innate and rare talents, so we need role models even more.

Michael Jordan is a gifted basketball superstar and a hero, but he isn't a role model. Mickey Mantle is still a hero to at least two generations of baseball fans, but he is not a role model. Michael

Jackson, brilliant performer that he is, is not a role model, either. These are three supremely talented individuals we revere, but we can't completely relate to them. None of us can "be like Mike," as the Nike commercial advises, and too often our kids feel a sense of failure when that reality hits home. Michael Jordan flies on the wings of almost superhuman talent, but how many kids can realistically expect to fill his shoes?

UNREALISTIC ROLE MODELS

More than half of black children live in homes headed by women, and almost all of the black teachers they encounter are also women. This means that most African-American male children do not often meet black male role models in their daily lives. . . . Lacking in-the-flesh models, many look to TV for black heroes.

Unfortunately, TV images of black males are not particularly diverse. Their usual roles are to display physical prowess, sing, dance, play a musical instrument or make an audience laugh. These roles are enticing and generously rewarded. But the reality is that success comes to only a few extraordinarily gifted performers or athletes.

David L. Evans, *Newsweek*, March 1, 1993.

In our schools, in newspapers, on television and most especially in our homes we must work much harder to convey the message that being an "average American" isn't just an average accomplishment. It's an exceptional one.

Down every street and around every corner, there are role models in "ordinary" citizens who hold jobs, pay their bills and contribute to the honest progress of our country. The attorney next door is a role model because he can explain what it took to become who he is. The bank teller and postman on the job for 45 years are role models who do their part by putting food on the table and clothes on the backs of their children. We as parents and educators, media makers and policy creators, must dispel this million-dollar notion that unless you have a lot of money, you are a nobody. Let us identify role models and celebrate them. Let us all be role models, no matter what our profession is.

THE TRIUMPH OF BEING "AVERAGE"

In this time of great political promise, we as individuals must heed the call for a change in our attitudes toward our youth.

We must govern ourselves according to the fundamental principle that we are our children and our children are us. We must act as we would want them to. They have to understand the triumph in being an "average" member of our society.

Only then will we realize that it is the average American who makes this country great, and not the few heroes. And only then will America's children be able to lead us toward tomorrow's light.

"Each year in the United States thousands die and millions live in fear because of the perversity of TV programming."

REDUCING SEX AND VIOLENCE ON TELEVISION WOULD BENEFIT CHILDREN

Robert Posch

In the following viewpoint, Robert Posch maintains that the depiction of sex and violence on television can have a profoundly negative effect on children. Viewing repeated portrayals of violence on television desensitizes children to the pain and horror of real-life violence, he contends, and causes them to act out in aggressive ways. Posch believes that television violence must be reduced in order to lessen the destructive impact of such programming on children and society. Posch is vice president of legal affairs for Doubleday Book & Music Clubs, Inc., and the author of several books, including *The Complete Guide to Marketing and the Law*.

As you read, consider the following questions:

1. How many televised murders does the average child see by the time he or she graduates from elementary school, according to the American Psychological Association, as cited by the author?
2. To what other commercial product does Posch compare television programming?
3. According to the author, what absurd claim is made by television programmers concerning the effects of television violence versus those of advertising?

Excerpted from Robert Posch, "What You Do Emerges from Who You Are," *Direct Marketing* magazine, July 1993. (Footnotes in the original have been omitted.) Reprinted with permission from the author and Hoke Communications, Inc.

The fundamental premise of television is based on at least one of two lies. If a 15-second commercial can prompt the viewer to buy (or vote), the 25 acts of violence per hour will likewise prompt the targeted viewers to similarly respond with violence. If television does sell what it promises, television is much worse for society than all the illegal and legal drugs you could name. If this is not true, then all TV advertising is sold on a fraudulent premise and a lot of stupid marketers have bought a lot of dead air space from crooked TV marketing departments.

TELEVISION SELLS

More and more it is obvious that television does sell and all of America is the victim of the real junk medium.

As one expert [William H. Dietz] summed it up when testifying to Congress in 1993:

> The repeated denials by network executives that televised violence has no effect on the behavior of children or adolescents are inconsistent with the use of repetitive commercials to sell products. Children clearly respond to commercials. The inability of children to distinguish between commercial and program content led the Federal Trade Commission to require a break between cartoons and commercials. This decision recognizes that young children have difficulty distinguishing fantasy from reality. Therefore, we can expect no difference between the effect of a fantasy on human character or the development of early childhood behavior. It is illogical to argue that children will not also respond to the violence that they see, which occurs far more frequently on television than does any commercial.
>
> Both parents and broadcasters must be held responsible for the television that children see.

The primary medium [television] tears the culture asunder, ruins families and is undoubtedly the cause of much violence and murder in the United States. . . . Each year in the United States thousands die and millions live in fear because of the perversity of TV programming. . . .

[In May 1993] the most liberal members of the U.S. Congress grilled a number of TV executives for what even for them was a despicable television "sweeps" period.

Representative Edward Markey began lauding Senator Paul Simon's Television Violence Act of 1990 which

> gave all of us renewed optimism that the industry might begin to control the epidemic of violence on television. Yet three years later, we find ourselves in the throes of yet another "Prime-Time Crime Wave," as another way May Sweeps finds us mired in murder and mayhem.

Clearly the industry has not gotten the message. A study of just 10 channels by the Center for Media and Public Affairs found more than 1,800 violent acts during 18 hours of programming—more than 10 violent acts per hour. Other surveys of violence on television have found that the average network prime-time program contains five acts of violence, while the average network children's program contains 26 acts of violence.

Today the average child spends more time watching television than in the classroom. As a result, television has become an 'electronic teacher' for many children. The question we must answer today is this: If the electronic teacher delivers a daily dose of violent, antisocial behavior, what will happen to our children? And what will happen to our society?

What Is a Society For?

To ask this question is to explore the ultimate issue of any body politic. What is society for? Why do we need it? Does it matter how we define a society? What is its purpose in being? How shall it have social cohesion? How will it perpetuate itself in raising up the next generation?

These are the most basic questions, yet we never raise, much less examine them. Mindless mantras like "change" are an idiot's substitute. Until we ask the real questions that matter, we as people cannot judge whether policies we enact or tolerate are aimed in the right direction toward producing, if not a good, at least a sane and realistic society.

Little Optimism

Senator Paul Simon's testimony leaves little optimism for our future. Among his points:

Any parent knows that children imitate what they see and hear. . . . Numerous studies have addressed the question of just how much television our children are watching and how violent it is. I'd like to share with you some of the most recent findings:

It is estimated by the time youngsters graduate from high school, many of them will have watched television 22,000 hours, compared to only half that number spent in school. By 18, young people will have been exposed to as many as 18,000 televised murders and 800 suicides. (Fred Hechinger, Carnegie Council on Adolescent Development, 1992).

The American Psychological Association cited a similar statistic: The average child witnesses 8,000 murders by the time he/she graduates from elementary school and witnesses more than 100,000 assorted acts of violence (*Big World, Small Screen: The Role of*

Television in American Society, 1992).

Dr. Brandon Centerwall published one of the most shocking studies in the *Journal of the American Medical Association* on June 10, 1992. In it, he states that:

> Whereas infants have instinctive desire to imitate observed human behavior, they do not possess an instinct for gauging a priority whether a behavior ought to be imitated. They will imitate anything, including behaviors that most adults would regard as destructive and antisocial. . . . Up through ages three and four years, many children are unable to distinguish fact from fantasy in television programs and remain unable to do so despite adult coaching. In the minds of such young children, television is a source of entirely factual information regarding how the world works.

Dr. Centerwall concludes by saying: "Long-term childhood exposure to television is a causal factor behind approximately 10,000 homicides annually. . . . If hypothetically television technology had never been developed there would be 10,000 fewer homicides each year in the United States, 70,000 fewer rapes and 700,000 fewer injurious assaults."

Reprinted by permission of Ed Gamble.

That's a very powerful and hard to believe conclusion. But it was just as hard to believe the harm that cigarettes cause when medical researchers first came out with those studies years ago. Suppose the study is 50 percent off target. That still suggests that by changing our TV programming we could eventually prevent

5,000 murders a year, 35,000 rapes and 350,000 assaults. Even if the study is 90 percent wrong, we could save 1,000 of those murdered and prevent 7,000 rapes and 70,000 assaults each year, simply by changing our TV programming.

If cigarette companies are liable for cancer, people such as our television network presidents should be held personally accountable for the poison they peddle. Any victim (and we're all victims) should consider these deep pockets in a strict liability suit.

All of this begs the ultimate question: For what purpose are we raising children, anyway? Is it solely to be a self-absorbed consumer whose hedonistic lifestyle mirrors the sponsors of the junk entertainment? For those murdered by those incited by TV violence—this question is as removed from reality as their former physical existence here on earth.

POISON IN, POISON OUT

Our self-anointed enlightened opinion makers state that hours of sex- and violence-saturated videos make no impression on anyone (least of all children), but then argue how a 15-second TV spot sells soap or compels someone to switch his or her vote for president. Of course, they have demographic studies for each program's age range so they can be targeted. They specifically target impressionable people with their commercials and they know the targeted audience will actively respond to the stimulus.

Have you ever thought about the absurdity of programmers who smugly tell you that the thousands of violent assaults children witness on the tube have no impact? Talk about child abuse! We pour graphic violence, sex and vulgarity onto our young hour after hour, year after year. Particularly warping to young males is the combination of sex and violence (and often humor) to desensitize impressionable people to reality. You've all read the statistics of how many rapes, murders, slashings, etc., an impressionable child fills his or her subconscious with. The opinion elite then says that there is no price to pay! Ignore the objective statistical verification of the increase in violence paralleling the hours watched. Consider the duplicity in the assertions of advertising and programming. A 15-second commercial can prompt action behavior to buy, but 25 acts of violence an hour have no impact on behavior to assault! From what we do emerges who we are—a thought truly frightening.

Only a public deadened by the passivity of television could tolerate, much less believe, this distinction to be plausibly valid. We know a 15-second ad prompts action (or why are we buying it) and a mind programmed into the violence of the programs will also produce consequent acts. Worse than any narcotic, our addiction to gratuitous sex and pervasive violence means we need more and more of it to get our "fix." The programming on the TV set is for our era the substitute for the Roman Coliseum. Candidly, Martin Scorsese agreed: "Maybe we need the catharsis of bloodletting and decapitation like the ancient Romans needed it, as ritual, but not real like the Roman circus."

No one would debate our children (even the decadent Romans generally banned minors from the Coliseum) and adult population is much more violence-saturated than any other period of decadence in history. Decadence is defined as a society's inability or unwillingness to defend its core values. We can muster no sustained defense against TV programming's relentless assault against us individually or the very institutions on which our nation's moral claim is stated. From the assault of television, we are obviously a decadent nation. We are promoting violence and at the same time dulling and desensitizing our society toward violence in their daily interaction.

"*American adults . . . strongly favor two doable solutions—more job training for youth . . . and job placement.*"

JOB TRAINING CAN HELP TEENAGERS

Mary Rose McGeady

Mary Rose McGeady, a Catholic nun, is president of Covenant House, a shelter and aid organization for runaway and homeless teenagers. In the following viewpoint, McGeady states that job training programs can help wayward teens become self-sufficient and less of a burden on society. McGeady points to the success rate of Covenant House's job training and placement program as evidence that such programs improve the welfare of children.

As you read, consider the following questions:

1. What are the major problems facing at-risk youth, according to the 2,800 Americans polled by Yankelovich Partners, cited by the author?
2. How does having improved job skills affect teenagers, in McGeady's opinion?
3. What will be the consequences of decreasing public assistance for teenage unwed mothers, according to the author?

From Mary Rose McGeady, "'At Risk' Youths: How to Help," *Christian Science Monitor*, September 18, 1995. Reprinted by permission of the author.

In the time it takes to read this sentence, a child in America will drop out of school. In the time it takes to read this column, another child will run away and a teenage girl will have a baby.

The real horror is not the statistics themselves. It's the knowledge that behind each of these numbers is a real child. A child who cries like you and I do, who is as terrified as you and I would be if we walked in his or her shoes. Our streets are filled with these children. There are hundreds of thousands of them out there, lost, hungry, scared—alone. These are America's "at risk" kids.

I feel as though I know these children better than perhaps anyone. During my years as president of Covenant House, the country's largest child-care agency, 200,000 homeless and runaway youths have ended up on my doorstep.

In 1995, increasingly overwhelmed by the avalanche of these lost kids, I asked Yankelovich Partners, a national public policy research firm, to survey American adults' opinions of the problem. The results are disturbing.

AMERICANS SEE A CRISIS

According to the sampling of 2,800 Americans, 1 in every 2 adults personally knows a young person who could be labeled "at risk"—children unable to function normally in society. Americans increasingly feel this crisis where it hurts the most— in their neighborhoods and homes. Respondents said one-third of the 17- to 21-year-olds in the country fall into this at-risk category. One-fourth said there's a young person at risk in their own family. Not surprisingly, 69 percent cited drug abuse as a major problem. Sixty-three percent cited dysfunctional families and lack of job skills.

The scourge of drugs and the breakdown of the American family are complex ills that require long-term solutions. What's most encouraging about this survey, however, is that American adults said they strongly favor two doable solutions—more job training for youth (67 percent) and job placement (62 percent). This broad consensus is on target.

For almost a decade, Covenant House has considered job-skills education and assistance in the job search the key to developing a young person's self-respect and personal investment in the future.

At any one time in its New York City facility, Covenant House has more than 100 18- to 21-year-olds in our "Rights of Passage" job-skills program, which has a 63 to 70 percent success rate a year after training is complete.

Assistance Is Vital

Covenant House's success in this area is largely due to its partnership with the local business community, which has set up several of the training modules and assisted in job placement. Fully 70 percent of the single mothers who graduate from the program are still employed in good positions—living independently without resorting to public assistance—a year after graduation.

These statistics are all the more significant in light of proposals to reduce or eliminate support for under-18 single mothers. Without assistance, what hope can they have of ever gaining skills for the kinds of jobs that lead to independence?

A Successful Program

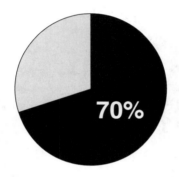

70%

Percentage of single mothers who are still employed one year after graduating from Covenant House's job skills program

Source: Mary Rose McGeady, *Christian Science Monitor*, September 18, 1995.

There is no evidence that doing away with welfare's small safety net will do anything but cause increased hardship for the young people and their infants. In the end, we will pay as a society through increased burdens on our medical and criminal-justice systems.

Eight of the 10 respondents to the survey said the country should be doing more to help at-risk young people. Four in 10 said the proposed reforms will offer less help to at-risk youth.

Clearly, we need to reform a system that has often encouraged dependence. Covenant House is one of many agencies, both private and government-supported, whose programs give young people a second chance to make it. Are our political leaders listening?

> "If we think in terms of a residential urban university that teaches everything from academics and job skills to how to be a good neighbor, you could transform lives."

RESIDENTIAL URBAN UNIVERSITIES CAN HELP TROUBLED CHILDREN

William Raspberry

William Raspberry is a syndicated columnist whose editorials appear in the *Washington Post* and other newspapers. In the following viewpoint, Raspberry presents the views of former Xerox executive Kent Amos, who advocates the creation of residential urban universities for children whose families are unable or unwilling to support them. According to Raspberry, such facilities could provide children with a place to stay temporarily when their families are in crisis and could offer education and job training.

As you read, consider the following questions:

1. In the past, how were children in difficult circumstances often cared for, according to Amos, as quoted by the author?
2. Why are many Americans averse to the idea of residential facilities for children, in Raspberry's opinion?
3. How does society usually respond to troubled young people, according to Amos, as quoted by Raspberry?

K ent Amos, having finished his remarks, had a question for the school principals in his audience.

"How many of you have children in your schools who really shouldn't go home? Stand up, please." Every principal in the room stood up.

Amos already knew what the principals were acknowledging—that most schools have at least a few students whose homes are not fit places for children. But he wanted to drive the point home.

"If you have as many as 10 percent of your kids who shouldn't go home, keep standing," he said.

Nobody sat down.

As he raised the ante to 20 percent, and then 30 percent and 40 percent, more and more of the principals took their seats. But, he told me later, at least a few were still on their feet in acknowledgement that as many as 80 percent of their students live in severely dysfunctional homes. Then:

"How many of you know about Newt Gingrich?" Everybody did. "How many of you agree with his proposal for orphanages?" Nobody did.

"Well, what do you propose to do with these kids who you say shouldn't go home? These are our kids, in our classrooms. Don't we need to go beyond criticizing Newt Gingrich and come up with a rational answer for these kids? You know very well that if we don't, a lot of them will die—and you can't blame their deaths on Gingrich."

A COMMUNITY FOR CHILDREN

Amos, a former Xerox executive, has made a virtual avocation of saving children from the perils of mean streets and dysfunctional families. His home has, for years, been their home: their haven for studying, inculcating values, thinking about their future. He now runs the Washington-based Urban Family Institute.

His purpose the other day was to tempt his audience to consider a vision he has had in his head for some time: of a community committed to its children, with institutions designed to further that commitment.

"When you and I were growing up," Amos explained later, "the child who got into difficult circumstances didn't have to leave the community. He was just taken in by neighbors until the situation cleared up.

"Now suppose these principals had some place within walking distance of the school where they knew they could send their troubled kids to stay for a while, where they would be taken care of by neighbors—where even the adults might get some help in sorting out their problems. There could be supervised study, recreation, everything—right in the neighborhood."

But first, he says, we need to get over our aversion to residential facilities for children, an aversion based on bitter memories of correctional institutions or such custodial facilities as the mercifully closed Junior Village in Washington. Such environments represent one possibility. Boarding schools represent quite another.

BUILDING A COMMUNITY

Children who need a clean, safe shelter often find better accommodations through private organizations than they do in government-supported shelters or public housing. . . . Many private shelters are being designed like communities, utilizing residents' skills to maintain or improve the building and grounds and daily routines. Teenagers are trained to do repair and maintenance work or run errands. Preteens baby-sit younger shelter children. . . . By working together and drawing on one another's skills, shelter people build a sense of pride in themselves and their community. Without the burden of government paperwork, private shelters have more flexibility to try novel approaches.

Eleanor H. Ayer, *Homeless Children*, 1997.

The second requirement, though, is to come up with the money to fund the sort of arrangement Amos has in mind.

"We have to think of problem-solving from a zero base," he says. "Assume there won't be any new money, and you get quickly to two ideas we're not used to dealing with: how to better spend the money you do have and how to develop a fund-out strategy—a plan for working people out of the system."

The neighborhood emergency residence is just a start. What he really envisions is a technically sophisticated campus-like setting with the express goal of moving young people from troubled childhood to responsible, independent adulthood.

GUIDANCE, NOT PUNISHMENT

"We never think of helping troubled young people to change their lives, by giving them the guidance and education and training they need. Instead, we think punitively: Three strikes and you're out, two years and you're off welfare—even if you have no place else to go.

"But if we think in terms of a residential urban university

that teaches everything from academics and job skills to how to be a good neighbor, you could transform lives. A single such university could accommodate children, families and single adults, with children spending some time with their families, some time in their own dorm.

"You might even convert a public housing complex into an urban family university, where residents—who would have to apply for the opportunity—could create their own safe and functional communities. There could even be a scheme by which they could move to owning their units . . ."

Amos will spin his dream as long as you care to listen, but his fundamental point is critical: Most public housing residents and welfare recipients don't like living the way they live; they just don't know how to make it better.

Instead of lapsing into political warfare over Newt Gingrich and orphanages, some of us might usefully spend time figuring out how to use available resources, not to subsidize dysfunction but to help people transform their lives.

"Often . . . a court-appointed
advocate is the single
consistent—and friendly—adult
presence in a child's life."

VOLUNTEER COURT ADVOCATES CAN
HELP CHILDREN

Elizabeth Mehren

Court-appointed special advocates, or CASAs, are volunteers
who gather information and act as advocates for children in the
juvenile justice and child welfare systems. In the following
viewpoint, Elizabeth Mehren maintains that CASAs are often the
only people who truly work in the child's best interests. Because
volunteer advocates are not burdened with the timetables and
large caseloads that lawyers and social workers must contend
with, she writes, they are able to devote adequate time to ensure
that each child in their care receives the attention he or she
needs. Mehren is a staff writer for the *Los Angeles Times*.

As you read, consider the following questions:

1. How did the idea for CASAs come about, as described by the
   author?
2. What is the "one ideal" goal of volunteer advocates,
   according to Gay Courter, quoted by the author?
3. What two threats do volunteer advocates face, according to
   Mehren?

Like so many people, Gay Courter felt a nagging need to do something for her community. She was a product of the '60s, an Antioch grad who clung to the quaint insistence that one person really could make a difference. But she was also a mom, wife, novelist and filmmaker. To her frequent dismay and occasional embarrassment, her idealism tended to get caught in the crunch.

Then Courter read about a 2-year-old whose stepfather had drowned him by shoving his head in a toilet. That did it. In October, 1989, Courter signed up to become a guardian ad litem—one of 37,000 people in all 50 states and the District of Columbia who volunteer as child advocates, shepherding kids through the maze of juvenile courts and the child welfare system.

Soon she was acting as bureaucratic quarterback for the girl she calls Lydia, a 16-year-old whose record said she had tried to kill her baby sister by cooking her in a microwave oven. (The sister was actually 10, and it was Lydia's boyfriend who, in a fit of teen-age bravado, had threatened to bake the girl alive.)

Courter took on the case of 15-year-old Sharhonda, who took to heart a social worker's careless comment that the best way to get Medicaid and food stamps was to get pregnant. She angrily did combat with Renata, a foster mother who evicted one of Courter's charges, but kept the boy's Christmas presents.

"My mission is pure: to make something that has gone terribly wrong a little better," Courter writes in I Speak for This Child, her chronicle of five picaresque years in the social welfare system. "Phone call by phone call, visit by visit, meeting by meeting, court appearance by court appearance," Courter recounts, she seeks to be a consistent presence in a child's life, a defender who represents nothing more than the best interests of the child.

Unpaid Champions of Children

Courter's home state, Florida, boasts one of the country's largest guardian ad litem networks. In California and elsewhere, these unpaid champions of children are known more often as CASAs, or court-appointed special advocates.

The idea of training volunteers to act on behalf of neglected, abused and abandoned children dates from 1976, when David Soukup, then a Superior Court judge in Seattle, worried that child welfare cases were railroaded through the system with little concern for a child's long-term interests. In Soukup's view, lawyers, judges and social workers—with caseloads of 60 or more children at one time—were too overburdened to attend to the complexities of each child's case.

"I was consumed by the fact that I didn't have enough information about each child, and I just didn't know if I had done the very best job I could," recalled Soukup, now a practicing attorney and CASA volunteer.

He agonized, for example, about "the 3-year-old girl who shows up in the hospital, and the physicians think she's been sexually abused. The mother says, 'No, she fell off the swing, and besides, my boyfriend, Bill, left last week.' So you go along with the mother's word, then six months later you pick up the paper and read that Bill's back and the girl's dead."

Soukup expected maybe four or five people to respond when he contacted local charitable groups about training volunteers to work with children in the courts. Instead, "50 or 60 people showed up. I knew I was onto something."

ONE CHILD AT A TIME

Today, court-appointed guardians watch over about one-quarter of the estimated half a million cases of children who are either awaiting adoption or living in foster homes, group homes or juvenile jails. Funding for their training and for the guardian program comes from state and federal sources.

But much like the stories of the children themselves, the program remains little known, said Michael Piraino, chief executive officer of the National Court Appointed Special Advocate Assn. in Seattle.

"These courts tend to be kind of invisible to most people. Most people don't want to know about them," Piraino said.

"They are difficult situations, ugly cases" that challenge the conventional, idealized view of the family as a happy, stable institution, Piraino said. An abused or neglected child is often trapped in limbo, he observed, wedged between parents who are unable to care adequately for a child—but also unprepared to say goodby—and a system that frequently falters at finding a safe, permanent home for that child.

"The way to change this is one child at a time," said Piraino, who experienced these frustrations as a lawyer in the social welfare system. "It's not theoretical, it's not ideological. It's knowing a lot about each kid who comes through the system—and . . . having the strength to make recommendations to a judge."

In Los Angeles, CASA volunteer Renne Bilson said much of the strength of her work comes from the amount of time she spends with each client. She has been working with one 14-year-old girl for 3½ years, a luxury afforded to few who make their living in the trenches of social welfare.

But Bilson's shortest case, four months, was also one of her tidiest. A 3-year-old boy was abandoned by his mother at a hospital. The child had only limited verbal skills, and no record in state or county welfare rolls. By "playing detective," Bilson tracked down a grandmother in Philadelphia within four months. The boy and his grandmother were reunited in court on Christmas Eve.

But most of her cases "are up and down," Bilson said. "And the resolutions are not miraculous, because we are not miracle workers."

Besides, she continued, the numbers are daunting. In Los Angeles County, "there are 50,000 children under the jurisdiction of the courts" at any one time, Bilson said. "There are 1,200 new cases per month." The Los Angeles CASA program has a corps of about 250 volunteers, "so we touch 1% to 2% of the kids."

"But for the kids that we do touch," she said, "it makes a difference."

MAKING A DIFFERENCE

Courter echoed that sentiment. "This is one situation where the cliché of making a difference really is true."

As rewarding as her efforts may be for any particular child—Lydia got her microwave rap expunged; Sharhonda and her baby got a home; Renata's ex-foster child got his Christmas cowboy boots back—"I do this for me," Courter said. "It's so satisfying."

At 50, Courter describes herself as someone who missed the demographic cutoff of baby boomerdom, but still bought into the philosophy. Most of her attempts at altruism were "tremendously unfulfilling and useless," she said. "I would sit around and calculate how 10 high-powered women were wasting 30 hours and the whole weekend to raise $300 at a bake sale when the profit was $100."

Working as a guardian drew on her organizational skills, as well as her ability to use resources, Courter said. While honoring confidentiality at all times, "Guardians are expected to work outside the system, to cross certain boundaries. Independent thinking is encouraged."

Often, she said, a court-appointed advocate is the single consistent—and friendly—adult presence in a child's life. Social workers come and go and are constrained, moreover, by the unpleasant truth of bureaucratic quotas. Parents may be in jail, on drugs or otherwise unsuited for the job of caring for their children. Many such children bounce from one transitional living facility to another, racking up what Courter calls "file drawers filled with tears and pain."

"There is only one ideal here," she said, "and that is a safe, permanent home for every child, as quickly as possible."

Courter would like a cap on the time a child can spend in foster care. In some cases, she believes birth parents should consign primary rights to their child's custodial family, while retaining visitation and communication rights.

FINDING THE TIME TO VOLUNTEER

Surely, there are times in everyone's life when our personal resources are so depleted that we have nothing left to give. . . . But the general complaint, "I'm too busy, I don't have the time," doesn't cut it with me anymore. Having spent 14 years in social service, as a professional and a volunteer, I know too many examples of people with busy, complicated lives who do find the time. . . . These are everyday people who've made community a priority. I wish more would do the same.

Julie Rindfleisch Granville, *Newsweek*, July 8, 1996.

"As a society, we have to say that the manifest best interest of a child is a basic entitlement," she said. "When these interests are in conflict with the interests of the parent, or the interests of the state, the child's interests should prevail."

But while no doubt noble, such goals are not so easily attained, said Eve Brooks of the Washington, D.C.–National Assn. of Child Advocates. "We need to have the structures in place that deal with the policies that help kids." High on the list of structures, she said, is representation.

In that capacity, court-appointed advocates "are fine—if they are assisting lawyers," Brooks said. "They are not fine if their primary function is to fill a gap."

And guardians face a constant threat of burnout on the one hand and emotional overattachment on the other. Noting that he had served as a judge, a criminal attorney and at times, a witness, Soukup called his own five years as a volunteer "the most difficult thing I have ever done in a courtroom—and the most rewarding."

EMOTIONAL INVOLVEMENT

As he first molded the CASA program, Soukup said, some skeptics wondered if volunteers would not become too emotionally involved in their cases.

"If they don't get emotionally involved," Soukup replied, "we've got the wrong volunteers."

Bilson, in Los Angeles, agreed that "sometimes letting go is the hardest part."

And Courter said that "I'm a total failure" at emotional detachment. This level of absorption, she said, was a happy surprise. "I don't know just what it is that happens," she said. "It's unexpected and unplanned, but it's a connection."

Since most of her young charges have led lives whose sadness far exceeds their years, "I'm surprised that I'm still doing this with the same level of enthusiasm," Courter said. "But every time I make a phone call, I make a difference."

PERIODICAL BIBLIOGRAPHY

The following articles have been selected to supplement the diverse views presented in this chapter. Addresses are provided for periodicals not indexed in the *Readers' Guide to Periodical Literature*, the *Alternative Press Index*, the *Social Sciences Index*, or the *Index to Legal Periodicals and Books*.

Douglas J. Besharov	"Working to Make Welfare a Chore," *Wall Street Journal*, February 9, 1994.
Andrew Cherlin	"Making Deadbeat Dads Pay Up at Work," *New York Times*, December 30, 1993.
Lonnie K. Christiansen	"Broken Promises: Fighting for Child Support and Winning," *Family Circle*, February 1, 1996. Available from 110 Fifth Ave., New York, NY 10011.
Economist	"A Father's Case," April 1, 1995.
Barbara Ehrenreich	"Oh, Grow Up!" *Time*, November 4, 1996.
Wade F. Horn	"Putting Parents First," *Wall Street Journal*, May 28, 1993.
Jesse Jackson	"Our Children Cry for Caring, Not Revenge," *Los Angeles Times*, December 19, 1993. Available from Times Mirror Square, Los Angeles, CA 90053.
Hilary Dole Klein	"Allied Forces," *Los Angeles Times*, August 23, 1995.
Jeanne Lenzer	"Youth Liberation—a Call to Action," *Z Magazine*, February 1993.
Laura Mansnerus	"Collecting from Deadbeat Dads," *Good Housekeeping*, May 1996.
J. Madeleine Nash	"Fertile Minds," *Time*, February 3, 1997.
Cathy Rindner Tempelsman	"Dear Mom, Clear My Calendar," *Wall Street Journal*, August 20, 1993.
Gayle Pollard Terry	"Marian Wright Edelman: Crusading for Children with This Aggressive Defense Fund," *Los Angeles Times*, November 21, 1993.
Jack C. Westman	"The Rationale and Feasibility of Licensing Parents," *Society*, November/December 1996.

FOR FURTHER DISCUSSION

CHAPTER 1

1. Charles Murray argues that the rise in illegitimate births in recent years is the main cause of poverty and neglect experienced by many of the nation's children. Robert Scheer, on the other hand, maintains that children born to unwed mothers are harmed more by the label "illegitimate" than by the circumstances into which they are born. Based on your reading of these viewpoints, do you think the children of unmarried single mothers are generally less advantaged than the children of married couples? Explain your answer.

2. Some commentators argue that children are better off when their unhappily married parents divorce. Others, including Steven Waldman, insist that in most families the children's best interests are served if the parents stay together even if they are unhappy. Based on the viewpoints of Waldman and Randall Edwards, do you think parents should try to endure a bad marriage for the sake of their children? Why or why not?

3. After reading the viewpoints of Richard "Casey" Hoffman, Jeffery M. Leving, and Kathleen Parker, do you think the term "deadbeat dads" is a fair label for divorced fathers who do not make their child support payments? Why or why not? Do you think that fathers who cannot pay child support should be allowed to visit their children? Explain your reasoning.

CHAPTER 2

1. William J. Bennett maintains that reforming the welfare system will reverse the rise in out-of-wedlock births, which he believes contributes to the problems that confront America's children. Hugh B. Price and Thomas J. Osborne contend that the reforms recommended by Bennett will push more children into poverty. Whose argument is more persuasive, and why?

2. Nina Shokraii contends that parental rights laws are needed so that parents can exempt their children from educational programs that they deem objectionable. Bunnie Riedel insists that children need to be able to access certain programs without gaining their parents' consent. Which point of view is more compelling? Defend your answer by referring to the viewpoints.

3. Andrew Cherlin advocates an increased federal government role in enforcing the collection of child support from noncustodial parents. Brian Doherty argues that increasing the fed-

eral government's involvement will lead to excessive government interference in people's personal lives and will not benefit children. Based on these viewpoints, do you think the federal government should increase its efforts to enforce child support payments? Why or why not?

CHAPTER 3

1. Richard B. McKenzie acknowledges that the survey upon which he bases his viewpoint has some limitations. What are these limitations? Do you see any other possible limitations that the author does not cite? To what extent, if at all, do these limitations affect the persuasiveness of McKenzie's conclusions?

2. Hannah B. Lapp describes the experiences of the Stefan family in order to support her argument that child protective service workers have become excessive in their efforts to uncover cases of child abuse. Does Lapp's presentation of this story persuade you to agree with her assessment of the child protection system? Why or why not?

3. Robert F. Drinan argues that the United States should ratify the UN Convention on the Rights of the Child in order to ensure the protection of children around the world. Phyllis Schlafly maintains that U.S. ratification of the treaty would jeopardize the rights of American citizens. Based on these viewpoints, do you think the United States should ratify the treaty? Defend your answer by citing one or both of the viewpoints.

CHAPTER 4

1. Summarize Jack C. Westman's arguments in favor of licensing parents. Regardless of whether or not you agree with Westman, formulate an argument in opposition to Westman's viewpoint. After having completed this exercise, decide whether you think Westman's idea is a good one. Explain your reasoning.

2. Montel Williams argues that adults are failing to be good role models for young people. List three people whom you consider to be good role models for children and young adults. Explain why they are good role models. Name three bad role models and explain why they fail to qualify as good role models.

3. This chapter presents various ways in which society can improve the welfare of children. Which of these ideas have the most potential to affect children's lives? Why? Do you have any other suggestions on how society can help children? Discuss your ideas.

ORGANIZATIONS TO CONTACT

The editors have compiled the following list of organizations concerned with the issues debated in this book. The descriptions are derived from materials provided by the organizations. All have publications or information available for interested readers. The list was compiled on the date of publication of the present volume; names, addresses, phone and fax numbers, and e-mail and Internet addresses may change. Be aware that many organizations take several weeks or longer to respond to inquiries, so allow as much time as possible.

Administration for Children and Families
Children's Bureau
U.S. Health and Human Services Dept.
901 D St. SW, Washington, DC 20447
(202) 401-9215 • fax: (202) 295-9688
Internet: http://www.acf.dhhs.gov/programs/cb

The administration, part of the U.S. government, plans, manages, and coordinates nationwide assistance programs designed to promote stability, economic security, and self-support for families. It supervises programs and the use of funds to provide aid to the needy. The administration's website provides a wide range of child welfare information.

American Enterprise Institute (AEI)
1150 17th St. NW, Washington, DC 20036
(202) 862-5800 • information hot line: (202) 862-7158
fax: (202) 862-7177 • Internet: http://www.aei.org

AEI is a public policy institute that sponsors research and provides commentary on a wide variety of issues, including many that affect children, such as welfare reform, health care, and education. It publishes the bimonthly magazine *American Enterprise.*

American Humane Association (AHA)
Children's Division
63 Inverness Dr. East, Englewood, CO 80112-5117
(303) 792-9900 • fax: (303) 792-5333
e-mail: children@amerhumane.org
Internet: http://www.amerhumane.org

The American Humane Association, Children's Division, works to improve the quality of children's lives and to help public and private agencies respond effectively to the problem of child maltreatment. AHA provides training and education to protective service agencies, program evaluations of child protective service systems, and research, information, and publication services. Its publications include the quarterly journal *Protecting Children* as well as numerous books, brochures, fact sheets, and a video on the visual assessment of child maltreatment.

American Public Welfare Association (APWA)
810 First St. NE, Suite 500, Washington, DC 20002-4267
(202) 682-0100 • fax: (202) 289-6555

APWA is an organization of public welfare agencies and individuals interested in welfare issues, including how welfare and welfare reform affect children. The association supports two-year time limits on welfare benefits and favors federal block grants to states. Its publications include the quarterly newsletter *APWA News* and the quarterly journal *Public Welfare*.

American Youth Work Center (AYWC)
1200 17th St. NW, 4th Floor, Washington, DC 20036
(202) 785-0764 • fax: (202) 728-0657
e-mail: hn2759@handsnet.org

AYWC is an international citizens interest group concerned with juvenile justice and community-based youth services, including runaway shelters, hot lines, crisis intervention centers, drug programs, alternative education, and job training and placement. The center provides technical assistance to youth programs, serves as a clearinghouse and resource center, and sponsors training sessions, conferences, and a college internship program. It makes numerous publications and resources available to the public, and it publishes the bimonthly newspaper *Youth Today*.

Cato Institute
1000 Massachusetts Ave. NW, Washington, DC 20001-5403
(202) 842-0200 • fax: (202) 842-3490
e-mail: cato@cato.org

The institute is a libertarian public policy research organization that advocates limited government. It has published reports on numerous issues that affect children, including the welfare system, which the institute blames for creating generations of dependent children and mothers, in its quarterly *Cato Journal* and in its Policy Analysis series.

Child Welfare Institute (CWI)
Two Midtown Plaza, Suite 900, 1349 W. Peachtree St. NE,
Atlanta, GA 30309-2956
(404) 876-1934 • fax: (404) 876-7949
e-mail: acwi@aol.com

The Child Welfare Institute strives to develop the capability of human service agencies to assure the well-being of children, youth, and families through organizational development, training, and consultation. The institute publishes several books, including *From Foster Parent to Adoptive Parent, Mental Health Services for Children in Foster Care*, and *Assessing Attachment, Separation, and Loss*.

Child Welfare League of America (CWLA)
440 First St. NW, Suite 310, Washington, DC 20001-2085
(202) 638-2952 • fax: (202) 638-4004
e-mail: books@cwla.org • Internet: http://www.cwla.org

The Child Welfare League is an association of more than seven hundred public and private agencies and organizations devoted to improving the lives of children. CWLA publishes the journal *Child Welfare* six times a year, *Children's Voice* quarterly, and more than twenty books a year.

The Children's Foundation
725 15th St. NW, Suite 505, Washington, DC 20005
(202) 347-3300 • fax: (202) 347-3382
e-mail: cfwashdc@aol.com

The Children's Foundation works to improve the lives of children and those who care for them. It focuses on welfare reform, improving federal food assistance programs and child nutrition, establishing affordable day care, enforcing child support, and providing training to day care workers. The foundation publishes fact sheets, manuals, training materials, the bimonthly newsletter CF Childcare Bulletin and books such as Helping Children Love Themselves and Others.

Children's Safety Project
Greenwich House Inc.
27 Barrow St., New York, NY 10014
(212) 242-4140 • fax: (212) 366-4226

The Children's Safety Project benefits children who have been crime victims or witnesses to crimes or who are at risk for child abuse. Services include individual and family counseling and therapy groups and self-defense, personal safety, and crime avoidance classes for children. The organization publishes the collection of brochures Recognizing Child Abuse, which includes the titles Emotional Maltreatment, Physical Abuse, Sexual Abuse, and Neglect.

Family Research Council
801 G St. NW, Washington, DC 20001
(202) 393-2100 • fax: (202) 393-2134
Internet: http://www.frc.org

The council analyzes issues affecting the family and seeks to ensure that the interests of the traditional family are considered in the formulation of public policy. It lobbies legislatures and promotes public debate on issues concerning the family. The council offers numerous publications, including newsletters, reports, and books.

National Center for Missing and Exploited Children
2101 Wilson Blvd., Suite 550, Arlington, VA 22201-3052
(703) 235-3900 • (800) 843-5678 • fax: (703) 235-4067
TTY: (800) 826-7653
Internet: http://www.missingkids.org

Funded primarily by the U.S. Department of Justice, the center assists parents and citizen groups in locating and safely returning missing children. The center offers technical assistance to law enforcement agencies, coordinates public and private missing children programs, and maintains a database that coordinates information on missing children. It publishes several informational pamphlets on child protection and safety, and informational guides for babysitters and camp counselors, available from their website.

National Child Support Enforcement Association
444 N. Capitol St. NW, Suite 414, Washington, DC 20001
(202) 624-8180 • fax: (202) 624-8828
e-mail: ncsea@sso.org

The association promotes the enforcement of child support obligations and works to educate professionals and the public about child support issues. It facilitates the exchange of ideas among child support professionals and monitors legislation and regulations. The association publishes the quarterly newsletter *NCSEA News* and the reference book *Interstate Roster and Referral Guide.*

National Council for Adoption
1930 17th St. NW, Washington, DC 20009-6207
(202) 328-1200 • fax: (202) 332-0935
Internet: http://www.ncfa-usa.org

The committee includes individuals, agencies, and corporations interested in adoption. It supports adoption through legal and ethical means and advocates the right to confidentiality in adoption. The committee conducts research and conferences, provides information to the public, and supports pregnancy counseling, maternity services, and counseling for infertile couples. It distributes the Hotline Packet, a package of information regarding the adoption of children with special needs.

Welfare Law Center
275 Seventh Ave., Suite 1205, New York, NY 10001-6708
(212) 633-6967 • fax: (212) 633-6371
e-mail: hn0135@handsnet.org
Internet: http://www.afj.org/welflaw.html

The center is a nonprofit organization that works to ensure that adequate income support is available to meet the basic needs of the poor, including poor children. It publishes the monthly *Welfare Bulletin*, the bimonthly *Welfare News*, and the reports "Welfare Myths: Fact or Fiction? Exploring the Truth About Welfare" and "Out of the Arms of Mothers: What Will Happen to Children if Proposed Family Income Support Cuts Leave Some Parents Unable to Care for Them?"

Youth as Resources (YAR)
National Crime Prevention Council
1700 K St. NW, 2nd Floor, Washington, DC 20006-3817
(202) 466-6272 • fax: (202) 296-1356
Internet: http://www.weprevent.org

YAR believes that all youth—even those who feel they have little to give—possess talents, strengths, and skills that society needs and wants. The organization helps communities organize young people to design projects that will benefit the community. These projects include providing food for the homeless, renovating playgrounds, building homes for the poor, and performing anti–drug abuse puppet shows. YAR publishes fact sheets, the newsletter *Outlook*, and several videos describing the organization and its public counseling services.

BIBLIOGRAPHY OF BOOKS

Loren Acker, Bram Goldwater, and William Dyson — *AIDS-Proofing Your Kids: A Step by Step Guide*. Hillsboro, OR: Beyond Words Publishing, 1992.

Constance R. Ahrons — *The Good Divorce: Keeping Your Family Together When Your Marriage Comes Apart*. New York: HarperCollins, 1994.

Elizabeth Bartholet — *Family Bonds: Adoption and the Politics of Parenting*. Boston: Houghton Mifflin, 1994.

Jerome Beker and Douglas Magnuson, eds. — *Residential Education as an Option for At-Risk Youth*. Binghamton, NY: Haworth Press, 1996.

Mary Frances Berry — *The Politics of Parenthood: Child Care, Women's Rights, and the Myth of the Good Mother*. New York: Viking Press, 1993.

Douglas J. Besharov — *When Drug Addicts Have Children: Reorienting Child Welfare's Response*. Washington, DC: Child Welfare League of America, 1994.

Jan Blacher, ed. — *When There's No Place Like Home: Options for Children Living Apart from Their Natural Families*. Baltimore: Paul H. Brookes Publishing, 1994.

David Blankenhorn — *Fatherless America: Confronting Our Most Urgent Social Problem*. New York: BasicBooks, 1995.

Larry Brendtro, Martin Brokenleg, and Steve Van Bockern — *Reclaiming Youth at Risk: Our Hope for the Future*. Bloomington, IN: National Educational Service, 1993.

Margaret Brodkin and Coleman Advocates for Children and Youth — *Every Kid Counts: Thirty-One Ways to Save Our Children*. San Francisco: HarperCollins, 1993.

Robin Brown — *Children in Crisis*. New York: H. W. Wilson, 1994.

Katherine Cahn and Paul Johnson, eds. — *Children Can't Wait: Reducing Delays for Children in Foster Care*. Washington, DC: Child Welfare League of America, 1993.

Robert B. Cairns and Beverly D. Cairns — *Lifelines and Risks: Pathways of Youth in Our Time*. New York: Cambridge University Press, 1995.

Judith A. Chafel — *Child Poverty and Public Policy*. Lanham, MD: Urban Institute Press, 1993.

Colette Chiland and Gerald Young, eds. — *Children and Violence*. Northvale, NJ: Jason J. Aronson, 1994.

Children's Defense Fund — *Wasting America's Future: The Children's Defense Fund Report on the Costs of Child Poverty*. Boston: Beacon Press, 1994.

| Child Welfare League of America | *Homelessness: The Impact on Child Welfare in the '90s.* Washington, DC: Child Welfare League of America, 1991. |

Hillary Rodham Clinton — *It Takes a Village.* New York: Simon & Schuster, 1996.

William Damon — *Greater Expectations: Overcoming the Culture of Indulgence in America's Homes and Schools.* New York: Free Press, 1995.

Marilyn Davenport, Patricia Gordy, and Nancy Miranda — *Children of Divorce.* Milwaukee: Families International, 1993.

Madelyn DeWoody — *Health Care Reform and Child Welfare: Meeting the Needs of Abused and Neglected Children.* Washington, DC: Child Welfare League of America, 1994.

James Dobson and Gary Bauer — *Children at Risk: The Battle for the Hearts and Minds of Our Kids.* Wheaton, IL: Tyndale Press, 1994.

Marian Wright Edelman — *Guide My Feet: Prayers and Meditations on Loving and Working for Children.* Boston: Beacon Press, 1995.

James Garbarino et al. — *Children in Danger: Coping with the Consequences of Community Violence.* San Francisco: Jossey-Bass, 1997.

Irwin Garfinkel, Sara S. McLanahan, and Philip K. Robins, eds. — *Child Support and Child Well-Being.* Washington, DC: Urban Institute Press, 1995.

Joy Maugans Garland — *America's Throwaway Children: The Foster Care Dilemma.* Charlotte, NC: John Russell Publishing, 1990.

Susan Goodwillie, ed. — *Voices from the Future: Children Speak Out About Violence in America.* New York: Crown Publishers, 1993.

James P. Grant — *The State of the World's Children.* New York: Oxford University Press, 1993.

Judith M. Gueron and Edward S. Pauly — *From Welfare to Work.* New York: Russell Sage Foundation, 1991.

David A. Hamburg — *Today's Children: Creating a Future for a Generation in Crisis.* New York: Random House, 1994.

Irving B. Harris — *Children in Jeopardy: Can We Break the Cycle of Poverty?* New Haven, CT: Yale University Press, 1996.

Robert H. Haveman and Barbara L. Wolfe — *Succeeding Generations: On the Effects of Investments in Children.* New York: Russell Sage Foundation, 1994.

Donald J. Hernandez — *America's Children: Resources from Family, Government, and the Economy.* New York: Russell Sage Foundation, 1993.

Barbara Barrett Hicks	*Kids, Crack, and the Community: Reclaiming Drug-Exposed Infants and Children.* Bloomington, IN: National Educational Service, 1993.
Sheila B. Kamerman and Alfred J. Kahn	*Starting Right: How America Neglects Its Youngest Children and What We Can Do About It.* New York: Oxford University Press, 1995.
Jonathan Kozol	*Amazing Grace: The Lives of Children and the Conscience of a Nation.* New York: Crown Publishers, 1996.
Penelope Leach	*Children First: What Our Society Must Do—and Is Not Doing—for Our Children Today.* New York: Knopf, 1996.
Richard Louv	*Childhood's Future.* Boston: Houghton Mifflin, 1991.
Mary Briody Mahowald	*Women and Children in Health Care: An Unequal Majority.* New York: Oxford University Press, 1993.
Rebecca A. Maynard, ed.	*Kids Having Kids: Economic Costs and Social Consequences of Teen Pregnancy.* Washington, DC: Urban Institute Press, 1996.
Richard McKenzie	*The Home: A Memoir of Growing Up in an Orphanage.* New York: BasicBooks, 1996.
Marc Parent	*Turning Stones: My Days and Nights with Children at Risk.* New York: Harcourt Brace, 1996.
Nigel Parton	*Governing the Family: Child Care, Child Protection, and the State.* New York: St. Martin's Press, 1991.
Barbara A. Pine, Robin Warsh, and Anthony Maluccio, eds.	*Together Again: Family Reunification in Foster Care.* Washington, DC: Child Welfare League of America, 1993.
Valerie Polakow	*The Erosion of Childhood.* Chicago: University of Chicago Press, 1992.
Valerie Polakow	*Lives on the Edge: Single Mothers and Their Children in the Other America.* Chicago: University of Chicago Press, 1993.
David Popenoe	*Life Without Father: Compelling New Evidence That Fatherhood and Marriage Are Indispensable for the Good of Children and Society.* New York: Free Press, 1996.
Dona Schneider	*American Childhood: Risks and Realities.* New Brunswick, NJ: Rutgers University Press, 1995.
Richard Weissbourd	*The Vulnerable Child: What Really Hurts America's Children and What We Can Do About It.* Reading, MA: Addison-Wesley, 1996.
Edward Zigler and Susan Muenchow	*Head Start: The Inside Story of America's Most Successful Educational Experiment.* New York: BasicBooks, 1992.

INDEX

and need for caring climate, 112-13,
126, 139-40, 170
rights of, 129-30
and television viewing, 161
see also abuse of children; divorce;
orphanages; parents; poverty;
United Nations
Children's Defense Fund (CDF), 128,
149
Children Today, 35
child support, 39
enforcement of, 27, 35-36, 45, 51
and federalization, 73-74
benefits of, 69-71
ineffectiveness of, 38, 40, 72, 76
necessary to protect children,
33-36, 34, 35, 36, 53
unpaid, 33, 34, 35, 70
due to inability not irresponsibility,
38, 40, 41, 74-75
exaggeration about, 37
Child Support Recovery Act (CSRA),
35, 36
Christian Science Monitor, 167
City Limits, 55
Clinton, Bill, 28, 39, 45
and child support enforcement, 74
and health care reform plan, 58
and passing of welfare legislation, 54,
55
Clinton, Hillary, 61, 88, 128
Collins, James, 152
Colorado, 95
Commission on Quality Control (New
York state), 120
Congressional Budget Office, 19, 54
Connecticut, 70
Contract with America, 87
court-appointed special advocates
(CASAs), 172-77
as little-known program, 174
Courter, Gay, 172, 173, 175, 176, 177
Covenant House, 165-67
CQ Researcher, 71
cultural change, 46, 49, 52
see also morality

Dads Against the Divorce Industry
(DADI), 40
Department of Economic Development
(state), 75
Department of Social Services (state),
116
Dietz, William H., 160
DiIulio, John J., Jr., 51
divorce, 47, 156
amicable, 30-31
harmful effects on children, 25-28

can be minimized by parents, 29,
31-32
and politicians, 26, 28
should be discouraged, 27
see also child support
Doherty, Brian, 72
Donaldson, Sam, 26
Downey Side Families for Youth
Adoption Agency (New York City),
108
Drinan, Robert F., 122
drugs, 62, 84, 100, 144, 156

Early Childhood Development Act
(Missouri), 150
Edelman, Marian Wright, 128, 137, 149
Edwards, Randall, 29
Elementary and Secondary Education
Act, 154
England, 23
Equal Rights Amendment, 131
Evans, David L., 157
Even Start program, 149

Fagan, Patrick F., 62
family, 68, 99
education, 147
and fathers, 41, 48
absence of, 18, 23-24, 26, 48, 73
and importance of establishing
paternity, 35
irresponsibility of, 34
and need to be closer to children,
39
and need to learn responsibility,
76
importance of, 48, 51, 91, 154
see also children; illegitimacy; parents
Family Court, 75
Family Law Reform Act, 23
Family Preservation and Support
Services program, 153
Family Research Council, 47
Family Support Act (1988), 70, 73, 74
Fatherless America (Blankenhorn), 76
Federalist Papers (Hamilton), 22
No. 17, 50
Federal Trade Commission, 160
Fifield, Adam, 55
Fishman, Katharine Davis, 103
Fontana, Vincent, 119
Food Stamps, 20
foster-care system, 85, 97, 98, 109, 145
see also orphanages
France, 23, 53, 56, 57, 58

Galston, Bill, 26, 27
Gates, Bill, 59

New Jersey, 70
Newsweek, 28, 88, 157, 176
New York Times, 57-58
Nichols, Jerry, 35, 39
Nickman, Steven, 99
Novak, Michael, 48

Office of Alcohol and Drug Abuse
    Programs, 74
Office of Child Support (Vermont), 74,
    75
Of the People (parental rights group),
    61, 143, 147
Ohio University, 31
O'Neill, June, 19
Operation Non-Support (Florida), 38
orphanages, 169
    children can thrive in, 80-85
        academically, 82
        emotionally, 83
    costs of, 84, 90-91
    history of, 87-88
    negative aspects of, 86, 89-90
    see also adoption; foster-care system
Osborne, Thomas J., 53

Parental Rights and Responsibilities Act,
    60-63
parents
    incompetence of, 18
    licensing of
        would protect children, 142,
            145-147
    and need to retain authority, 62
    and parental rights laws, 64
        benefits of, 60, 61, 63
        damaging for children/teens, 66-67
        negatively affects education, 67-68
        opponents of, 61-62
        and Religious Right, 66
    role of, 65, 68
    selfishness of, 27
    see also children; divorce; family;
        Parents as Teachers; single-parent
        families
Parents as Teachers (PAT), 148, 149
    broad scope of, 149
    effectiveness of
        for children's education, 151-53
        federal recognition of, 153-54
        and home visits, 150
Parker, Kathleen, 37
Pavao, Joyce, 99
Personal Responsibility Act, 87, 88
Peter, Val J., 84
Piraino, Michael, 174
Playboy, 40
Popenoe, David, 48

Posch, Robert, 159
poverty, 18, 54, 138, 143
    of children in U.S., 34, 36, 55, 90, 141
        worse than other Western countries,
            57, 124-25, 126
    see also welfare system
Price, Hugh B., 53
Pride, Mary, 117
Progressive Policy Institute, 26
Psychology of Adoption (Brodzinsky and
    Schechter, eds.), 98

Quayle, Dan, 73

racial discrimination, 143
Raspberry, William, 168
Reagan, Ronald, 26, 28
    administration, 132
Rector, Robert, 48
Reinhard, John, 61, 62-63
Reno, Janet, 36
Republicans, 63, 87, 88
Riedel, Bunnie, 64
Roberts, Paula, 71
Rouse, Joy M., 148
Rowles, Gerald, 40
Rust, Donna, 105

Schechter, Marshall D., 100
Scheer, Robert, 21
Schlafly, Phyllis, 127
schools, 63, 131, 132, 157, 169
    provide more than education, 61
Science News, 95
Scorsese, Martin, 164
Search Institute (Minneapolis), 94, 96, 97
Senate Finance Committee, 18
Shalala, Donna, 128
Sharma, Anu R., 94, 96, 100
Shelby, Richard, 36
Shokraii, Nina, 60
Silver, Sheldon, 89
Simon, Paul (senator), 160, 161-62
Simon, Rita J., 98
single-parent families, 22, 70, 71
    increasing number of, 47, 73, 75
Slayton, Ann, 35
Society, 118, 146
Soukup, David, 173, 174, 176
Stand for Children event, 34, 35
Stefan, Billy, 116-18, 121
stereotypes, 39, 41, 73, 81, 93
    and use of slang names, 22
Stevenson, Adlai, 28

teenagers, 66, 67, 116, 138, 173
    and adoption, 93, 94-95, 97, 99, 100
    are worse off than ever, 47

job training can help, 165, 167, 170, 171
and pregnancy, 144-45, 156
risks for, 166
of HIV infection, 67
and suicide, 46
see also children; urban universities
television, 47, 49, 156, 157, 159
negative effects of, 140
and selling, 160, 163
violence caused by, 160-64
Television Violence Act of 1990, 160-61
Texas, 98
Teyber, Edward, 31
Theodore, Nikolas, 54
Thurow, Lester C., 59
Time magazine, 152
Turque, Bill, 28

United Nations
Committee on the Rights of the Child, 124
Convention on the Rights of Children, 68, 123, 124, 130
is unconstitutional, 128-29, 133
and U.S. ratification
desirability of, 122, 125-26
as threat to freedom, 127-32
General Assembly, 123, 125
International Children's Emergency Fund (UNICEF), 124
Secretary-General, 133
United States, 23, 56, 70, 123
adoption in, 93, 106
Congress, 20, 36, 50, 61, 160
funding for family programs, 153, 154
Constitution, 129, 130, 133, 144
Department of Education, 131
Department of Health and Human Services, 113
foreign perspective on, 58-59
and bias against Americans, 132
Justice Department, 40
and child-support enforcement, 35, 36
outlook for future, 46
Supreme Court, 94
and television-induced violence, 162
welfare spending in, 50

see also poverty
University of California-Berkeley, 106
University of Maryland, 98
University of Minnesota, 97
University of Southern California, 30
University of Wisconsin, 40, 54
Urban Family Institute, 169
Urban Institute, 55
Urban League, 54
urban universities, 168
are needed
to provide guidance/education, 171
to replace community networks, 169-70
USA Today magazine, 84

Vachss, Andrew, 110
Victims of Child Abuse Laws (VOCAL), 116
volunteers. *See* court-appointed special advocates

Waiting Child (TV show), 109
Waldman, Steven, 25
Washington Post, 58
Weld, William, 19
welfare system, 19
European, 56-57, 59
reform of
harmful consequences of, 54, 57
due to exaggerated individualism, 59
for foster care, 55
ignores shortage of jobs, 54
need for, 19-20
will benefit children, 45, 50-52
Westman, Jack C., 142
White House Conference on Children, 88
Will, George, 58
Williams, Montel, 155
Williams, Walter E., 19
Wilson, Pete, 22
Wisconsin, 95
Women with Infant Children (WIC), 20

Yankelovich, Daniel, 49

Zuflacht, Linda, 109